SpringerBriefs in Health Care Management and Economics

Series Editor

SpringerBriefs present concise summaries of cutting-edge research and practical applications across a wide spectrum of fields. Featuring compact volumes of 50 to 125 pages, the series covers a range of content from professional to academic. Typical topics might include:

- A timely report of state-of-the art analytical techniques
- A bridge between new research results, as published in journal articles, and a contextual literature review
- A snapshot of a hot or emerging topic
- An in-depth case study or clinical example
- A presentation of core concepts that students must understand in order to make independent contributions

SpringerBriefs in Health Care Management and Economics showcase emerging theory, empirical research, and practical application in health care, health economics, public health, managed care, operations analysis, information systems, and related fields, from a global author community. Briefs are characterized by fast, global electronic dissemination, standard publishing contracts, standardized manuscript preparation and formatting guidelines, and expedited production schedules.

Anna Bastone

The Power of Generative Artificial Intelligence for Value Co-Creation in Healthcare

Insights from Inter-Organizational Networks

Springer

Anna Bastone
Department of Management Studies and Quantitative Methods
University of Naples "Parthenope"
Napoli, Napoli, Italy

ISSN 2193-1704 ISSN 2193-1712 (electronic)
SpringerBriefs in Health Care Management and Economics
ISBN 978-3-032-14297-9 ISBN 978-3-032-14298-6 (eBook)
https://doi.org/10.1007/978-3-032-14298-6

This Springer imprint is published by the registered company Springer Nature Switzerland AG
The registered company address is: Gewerbestrasse 11, 6330 Cham, Switzerland

To my family, Simone and my friends.
I love you all more than words can say.

Foreword

The integration of technology and healthcare innovation is a challenging topic in several medical fields, including Precision Medicine. Notably, hospitals, R&D centres, and healthcare networks are widely adopting AI-based tools, wearable devices, and digital platforms. Thus, in healthcare, there is an inclination to adopt innovative technologies to maximise value for all the stakeholders. In this context, Generative Artificial Intelligence (GenAI) has emerged as a lever to optimise resource allocation, preserving the centrality of patient needs in line with the key principles of personalised, predictive, and preventive medicine.

This book summarises the main research carried out by Anna Bastone over the past years. The book is organised into four chapters.

Chapter 1 investigates inter-organisational networks and their formation process. Particularly, it provides a taxonomy of the main types of inter-organisational networks, describing how they are structured, the motivations and benefits behind their development, and how collaboration and knowledge exchange drive the co-creation of value.

Chapter 2 analyses the phenomena of digitalisation and AI in healthcare, focusing on how GenAI enhances efficiency, patient-centricity, and innovation.

Chapter 3 explores care networks in the context of oncological Precision Medicine. Particularly, it analyses the organisational, technological, and clinical dimensions of them, describing the main networks developed in Italy.

Chapter 4 describes the empirical analysis and the conceptual framework developed, identifying how GenAI acts as both an enabler and a potential barrier in healthcare networks.

The work done by Anna Bastone is a fascinating contribution to understanding how technological innovation, as GenAI, can transform healthcare networks, enhancing value co-creation.

I encourage Anna to continue her research and never lose her passion and enthusiasm.

Naples, Italy
September 2025

Francesco Schiavone

Preface

As the philosopher Heraclitus affirmed, "*the only constant in life is change*", proposing that the stability that human societies often pursue is transitory. This contradiction is particularly evident in the realm of technological innovation, where digitalisation and new technologies are reshaping the value creation process. Indeed, the current socio-economic panorama is characterised by technological change, which not only boosts existing processes, but also destabilises structures, requiring new strategies of adaptation.

Thus, companies are bound to rethink their value propositions and strategies. On the other hand, innovating often entails significant costs, not only material but also cultural and organisational. In this context, managing innovation turns out to be a driver of competitiveness and sustainability.

The healthcare sector represents a fertile ground in which to examine these dynamics. Indeed, shifting from volume-driven to value-based models implies the adoption of digital technologies to support new paradigms of care delivery. Precision Medicine (PM) is qualified as one of the main expressions of this transition.

In this context, GenAI emerges as a pivotal innovation because of its ability to generate new content, models, and solutions. Its application in healthcare revolutionises care delivery, personalising treatments, accelerating the development of therapeutic protocols, and reducing time-to-market for new drugs.

As Heidegger stated, "*technology is not just a means. It is a way of revealing*". Thus, this book sees GenAI as a new way to reveal novel possibilities for conceiving, organising, and delivering care, while simultaneously raising questions of governance, accountability, and ethics. In alignment with Porter and Teisberg's (2006) paradigm of value-based healthcare, the analysis underscores the need to reconfigure healthcare systems as ecosystems of co-created value. Here, GenAI is not examined merely as a technological artefact but as an institutional and organisational enabler that reshapes practices, relationships, and governance mechanisms.

This book synthesises the results of 4 years of research activity devoted to investigating the relationship between digital technologies, value creation, and inter-organisational healthcare networks. It was a stimulating and satisfying voyage during which I interacted with several stakeholders in the healthcare ecosystem.

Their visions, enthusiasm, and expertise made my research deeply meaningful, further fuelling my curiosity and passion for these topics.

Additionally, I also had the honour of receiving valuable suggestions from colleagues who share the same passion for exploring the managerial and organisational implications of digital transformation in healthcare.

I would like to express my deepest gratitude to Professor Francesco Schiavone from the University of Naples Parthenope, whose supervision and support have been, and continue to be, precious throughout my research journey. I am also grateful to Professor Christopher L. Tucci from Imperial College, who welcomed me during my visiting period. His enthusiasm and creativity were a stimulus, encouraging me to strive to do more. I would also like to extend my heartfelt thanks to my colleague Luigi Mosca from Imperial College for his warm welcome during those months in London and for his dedicated commitment to academic research.

I am grateful to Gaetano Cafiero and Stefano Tagliaferri from Kelyon Srl for welcoming me into their company with professionalism and kindness, as well as to Dr. Umberto Malapelle and Dr. Nicola Normanno, who dedicated their time to me during the preliminary interviews.

Furthermore, I wish to acknowledge the invaluable support of Nitza Jones (Springer New York) throughout the book proposal review and editorial process. I would like to express my sincere gratitude to the Associazione Filippo Adipietro for their invaluable support in developing my research activities

Special thanks also go to Professors Francesco Calza, Francesca Perla, Michele Simoni, Marco Ferretti, Giorgia Rivieccio, and Daniele Leone from the University of Naples Parthenope. I would also like to recognise my colleagues and friends Annaluce Mandiello, Giuseppina Marotta, Anna Pia Di Iorio, Erika Rescigno, and Michele Costagliola Di Fiore, whose encouragement, support, and love have accompanied me during this incredible journey.

Naples, Italy
September 2025

Anna Bastone

Competing Interests The author has no competing interests to declare that are relevant to the content of this manuscript.

Contents

About the Author

Anna Bastone is a Research Fellow in Management at the Department of Management and Quantitative Studies, University of Naples "Parthenope", where she also earned her PhD in Entrepreneurship and Innovation. Her research explores Performance Measurements, Big Data, Artificial Intelligence, Digital Transformation, and Healthcare Management. Additionally, she collaborates with VIMASS, the university's research lab for innovation and healthcare management (https://disaq.uniparthenope.it/vimass/).

Chapter 1
Developing a Taxonomy of Inter-organisational Networks

Abstract This chapter reviews the main literature on inter-organisational networks, highlighting the main factors driving their formation. By developing a comprehensive taxonomy, the chapter seeks to enhance understanding of how companies collaborate to sustain competitive advantage through ongoing innovation and value maximisation. The chapter concludes with a focus on Service-Dominant Logic, a key theoretical framework in the literature on value co-creation within inter-organisational networks. Particularly, the author underscores the relevance of interactions and relationships as the foundation for value co-creation and the involvement of stakeholders.

Keywords Inter-organisational network · Taxonomy · Formation process · Value · Service dominant logic

1.1 Defining Inter-organisational Network

Literature has extensively addressed inter-organisational network (Hagedoorn, 1993; Hergert & Morris, 1988; Mowery, 1988; Powell, 1996) since it has had a profound impact on several industries, such as (1) high-tech, (2) biotechnology, (3) the software industry, and (4) automotive. Particularly, the US electronics industry, the Japanese keiretsu (Steers et al., 1989) and the regional industrial districts in the Italian textile sector (Brusco, 1982; Ebers, 1997; Mariotti & Cainarca, 1986) are some of the most frequently mentioned instances of inter-organisational cooperation.

A unique definition of inter-organisational network is still lacking in the current body of knowledge. Nevertheless, it generally refers to *"a set of nodes and links that represent a relationship, or lack thereof, between nodes"* (Brass et al., 2004). Instead, authors such as Barringer and Harrison (2000) narrow the network, defining it as a *"constellation of organisations that come together through social contracts or agreements rather than legally binding contracts"*.

A. Bastone, *The Power of Generative Artificial Intelligence for Value Co-Creation in Healthcare*, SpringerBriefs in Health Care Management and Economics, https://doi.org/10.1007/978-3-032-14298-6_1

Notwithstanding, three common features qualify inter-organisational networks: (1) social interaction, (2) relationships, (3) connectedness, (4) collaboration, (5) collective action, (6) trust, and (7) cooperation (Provan et al., 2007, p. 480). Additionally, networks can be classified based on the *"function"* they perform (Popp et al., 2014).

Particularly, a network can perform three main functions: (1) information dissemination and knowledge sharing (McGuire, 2006; Milward & Provan, 2006), (2) network learning (Borgatti & Foster, 2003; Knight, 2002), and (3) innovation (Borgatti & Foster, 2003; Keast et al., 2004).

Notably, knowledge is crucial for innovation, and inter-organisational networks play a key role in sharing and adapting it (Carlsson, 2003; Hale, 2011). Particularly, innovation inside networks is driven by several actors and perspectives, making a culture of knowledge sharing and learning essential for success (Keast et al., 2004; Popp et al., 2014). The following paragraphs will describe different types of inter-organisational networks.

1.2 Type and Definition of Inter-organisational Networks

Although inter-organisational networks share common characteristics, they may differ in structures, goals, and governance. Thus, discovering similarities and differences among them can provide a lens through which to capture how organisations collaborate, share resources, and reach common goals. The following sections provide an overview of the main network models, emphasising their features, functions, and applications.

1.2.1 Strategic Alliance

Strategic alliances—one of the most common forms of inter-organisational collaboration—are defined as *"agreements between two or more organisations to share resources, expertise and knowledge in pursuit of common goals"* (Elmuti & Kathawala, 2001). Particularly, these agreements smooth collaboration between firms in (1) developing new technologies (Whipple & Frankel, 2000), (2) entering new markets, and (3) leveraging complementary strengths (Teece, 1986). Additionally, they allow for an expertise exchange by mitigating risk and expediting innovation (Gomes-Casseres, 1997). Moreover, through knowledge sharing, strategic alliances foster mutual learning and innovation. However, transmitting complex or tacit knowledge may need dedicated resources, such as skilled employees and shared infrastructure (Hamel et al., 1989).

Despite that, alliances are not without risks, including potential opportunistic behaviour (Das & Rahman, 2010). To mitigate it, firms must implement strong protective measures to control information flows and to establish clear boundaries around sensitive knowledge and strategic assets (Hamel, 1991).

1.2.2 Supply Chain Networks

Inter-organisational networks are widely discussed in the supply chain management literature (Christopher, 1992; Croom et al., 2000), due to the inherent complexity of interactions and interdependencies that are intrinsic to supply chains. Based on that, Lambert et al. (1998, p. 2) attested that supply chains are *"not a chain of firms with one-to-one relationships, but a network of firms and relationships"*. Thus, the network model can impact many aspects of the supply chain, such as innovation, performance, and the supply and distribution of goods and information (Borgatti & Foster, 2003).

Literature classified supply chain networks as (Knoke & Yang, 2019): (1) *Egocentric networks*, focused on a single actor and the social interactions and (2) *Complete networks*, which analyse the structure of the network, considering as many actors as possible (Knoke & Yang, 2019). These kinds of networks have benefits and risks. Particularly, collaboration can lead to cost reduction, increased market receptiveness, and revenue growth. However, it is also associated with high implementation, integration, and maintenance costs (McLaren et al., 2002).

1.2.3 Innovation Ecosystem

Innovation is crucial for economic growth and success. Its complexity needs a distinctive set of skills and a pattern of tools, methods, and processes (Tidd & Thuriaux-Alemán, 2016). Therefore, interactions between many actors become essential, paving the way to innovation ecosystems (Carayannis et al., 2018), defined as *"collaborative arrangements in which firms combine their offerings into a coherent, customer-focused solution"* (Adner, 2006). In this context, globalisation emphasised the role of territories as levers of competitive advantage. Thus, literature discussed Local Innovation Systems (LIS), where innovation is a systemic and interactive process emerging from interactions between heterogeneous actors geographically close (Cooke et al., 1998; Doloreux, 2002).

A different body of knowledge addressed the open innovation model (Chesbrough, 2003), which proposes to exploit both internally generated ideas and those from outside to push innovation and support economic growth (Bigliardi et al., 2021). Thus, it allows companies to stay competitive by harnessing external resources in an *ever-changing* market environment (Chesbrough & Appleyard, 2007). However, implementing it requires careful management of knowledge flows through practices that may include paid or free collaboration.

1.2.4 Technological Cluster

As mentioned before, geographical proximity is fundamental in fostering collaborative network development, particularly in the high-tech sector (e.g., Silicon Valley). Thus, technology clusters emerged, defined as *"a network of geographically concentrated interrelated firms and related institutions, operating in specific fields where they compete and co-operate, linked by elements of sharing and complementarity"* (Porter, 2000). Notably, tacit or complex knowledge transfer is facilitated by close and frequent interaction (Granovetter, 1992). Furthermore, proximity and frequency of interaction can foster the development of trust, affecting firms' willingness to share knowledge (Von Hippel, 1987).

In the context of technology clusters, technology spillovers are extensively discussed, referring to the mechanisms of both the entrenchment or immobility of knowledge and the diffusion of knowledge beyond the boundaries of the organisation or region where it was generated (Döring & Schnellenbach, 2006). Particularly, they occur when the benefits of a firm's research activities spill over to other firms through positive network externalities (Jaffe et al., 1993).

1.3 Inter-organisational Network Formation Process

Forming inter-organisational networks is one of the most discussed topics in the literature (Doz, 1996; Glaister & Buckley, 1996; Gray, 1985; Larson, 1992; Oliver, 1990; Ring & Van de Ven, 1994) and various approaches and theories have been used to explain why, how, and when such networks are formed (see Table 1.1).

Table 1.1 Theories to explain inter-organisational network formation

Authors	Theory	Why do inter-organisational networks emerge?
Coase (1988), Williamson (1975), and Williamson and Winter (1993)	Transaction cost	Inter-organisational networks allow companies to minimise transaction costs and uncertainty by creating a stable agreement between organisations (Rossignoli et al., 2015)
Barney (2001) and Penrose (1959)	Growth of the Firm and Resource Based-View	Inter-organisational networks enable companies to grow by combining their resources and capabilities to expand operations and markets (Baraldi et al., 2012)
Pfeffer and Salancik (2015)	Resource Dependence	Organisations create inter-organisational networks to reduce their dependence on external resources (Baraldi et al., 2012; Biermann & Harsch, 2017; Ebers, 1997)
Scott (2004) and Zucker (1987)	Institutional Theory	Organisations form networks to gain legitimacy and social support. They do so in accordance with prevailing institutional norms and values (Ebers, 1997; Grandori & Soda, 1995)
Argyris and Schön (1997) and Bandura (1977)	Social Learning and Organisational Learning	Networking is influenced by observational learning and the sharing of resources, which in turn reinforces organisational learning. This creates a continuous cycle of mutual exchange and growth (Beeby & Booth, 2000; Westerlund & Rajala, 2010)

Source(s): Author research

Particularly, focusing on the motivations behind network formation, several authors in organisational literature have attempted to categorise them. Ebers (1997), for instance, pinpoints two key *"sets of motivations"* including increased revenues and reduced costs, which therefore lead to reduced risks. Indeed, through networking, companies can cut competition or collectively confront familiar competitors. Additionally, networks enable one or more business activities to be carried out jointly, guaranteeing economies of scale or scope. The author, therefore, distinguishes *"three substantive dimensions"* pushing organisations to collaborate at the micro level: (1) resource flows and activity linkages, (2) trust and mutual expectation flows, (3) information flows (Ebers, 1997). Table 1.2 summarises their main characteristics.

Additionally, Oliver (1990) identifies six contingencies—that is, necessity, asymmetry, reciprocity, efficiency, stability, and legitimacy—facilitating or constraining inter-organisational networks formation. Based on this, Gray (1985) underlines the relevance of shared perceptions of legitimacy and power as foundational for network formation. On the other hand, Glaister and Buckley (1996) distinguish between institutional factors and relational ones, stressing that both the broader socio-economic context and the quality of pre-existing relationships meaningfully outline the probability and nature of network formation.

Based on these premises, one of the critical points is: *What are the steps in the process of inter-organisational network formation?* In this context, the formation process can be categorised as either *sequential* (Gray, 1985; Larson, 1992) or *cyclical* (Doz, 1996; Ring & Van de Ven, 1994).

Most literature on sequential processes identifies three developmental stages: (1) a *pre-networking* phase, where shared problems and relationship foundations are set; (2) a *relationship-building* phase focused on creating a common purpose; (3) a *structuring* phase where the network is formalised and its effectiveness evaluated (Gray, 1985; Larson, 1992). Conversely, promoters of cyclical processes suggest that *"networking involves a continuous and repeated process of negotiating mutual expectations, commitments to future actions, and the performance of those commitments, evaluated in terms of fairness and efficiency"* (Ring & Van de Ven, 1994).

Table 1.2 Micro-dimensions influencing the formation of inter-organisational networks

Dimension	Inter-organisational networking
Resource flows and activity links	By coordinating resources and activities, firms can: (1) access complementary resources; (2) reduce costs; (3) share non-codifiable knowledge; (4) manage uncertainty in the presence of high stability and predictability of resource flows
Trust and mutual expectations flow	How actors perceive the opportunities and risks of cooperation depends on mutual trust and expectations
Informations flow	Information sharing reduces communication costs, reduces uncertainty, and improves coordination. It also reduces asymmetry, aligning goals and solving conflicts

Source(s): Author research

Thus, Gulati and Gargiulo (1999) offer a systemic perspective, highlighting how exogenous and endogenous factors interact to influence the formation of inter-organisational networks (Fig. 1.1).

Among endogenous factors are: (1) *Relational embeddedness*—it is referred to the strength and quality of direct, cohesive relationships and ties between network actors that boost trust-building; (2) *Structural embeddedness*—related to the indirect ties that result from interactions between firms through familiar third parties; (3) *Positional embeddedness*—referred to the position an organisation occupies within the overall network of collaborations. According to the authors, the previous networks drive future collaboration by minimising the costs of searching for potential partners and mitigating the risk of opportunism. An exogenous factor is *strategic interdependence*, related to how strategically interdependent organisations are, such as through sharing critical resources or common goals.

Finally, *structural differentiation* regarding the firms' different roles and relationship profiles is central. Organisations shape a network's structure, which significantly influences future partnerships.

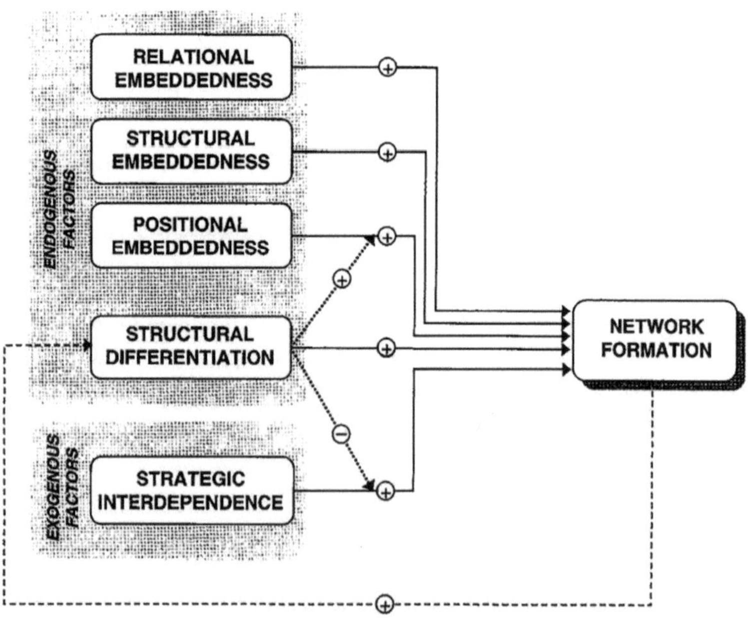

Fig. 1.1 The endogenous dynamic of the inter-organisational network. Source(s): Gulati, R., & Gargiulo, M. (1999). Where do interorganizational networks come from? *American Journal of Sociology*, 104(5), 1439–1493

1.4 Analysing Value-Creation in Inter-organisational Networks: The Service-Dominant Logic Theory

It is imperative to examine the mechanisms through which value is generated in inter-organisational networks. In this manner, the connections among all the players are essential to market survival and, consequently, to value generation, particularly in the service industry. Vargo and Lusch's (2004) *Service-Dominant Logic* (S-D Logic) is a seminal paradigm employed to describe value co-creation from an ecosystem perspective. By offering an alternative to conventional transaction logic, it advances knowledge of the value-generating process. The fundamental concept is a *"shift towards a service economy"*, in which value is created via the exchange of mutually beneficial and interdependent services rather than material things (Vargo & Lusch, 2014).

Thus, the value derives from a collaborative creation process in which participants simultaneously assume the roles of both producers and consumers. The resources contributed by each player are incorporated into the process of creating value. The beneficiary's role, as the consumer or end-user, is of vital importance in the value co-creation process due to their constant activity in establishing value based on their own experiences, needs, context, and perceptions. Furthermore, Service-Dominant Logic emphasises the pivotal role of institutions, including norms, regulations, and symbols, in promoting value co-creation within ecosystems (Sinton, 2020).

These ecosystems, where actors integrate resources and exchange services, are coordinated by shared institutional logic. Value, therefore, does not arise from a dyadic relationship between producer and consumer but from a network of interconnected actors collaborating to create and exchange value in a service-oriented context, giving rise to *"value constellations"* (Vargo & Lusch, 2008a, 2008b).

References

Adner, R. (2006). Match your innovation strategy to your innovation ecosystem. *Harvard Business Review, 84*(4), 98.

Argyris, C., & Schön, D. A. (1997). Organizational learning: A theory of action perspective. *Reis, 77/78*, 345–348.

Bandura, A. (1977). *Social learning theory*. Prentice-Hall.

Baraldi, E., Gressetvold, E., & Harrison, D. (2012). Resource interaction in inter-organizational networks: Foundations, comparison, and a research agenda. *Journal of Business Research, 65*(2), 266–276.

Barney, J. B. (2001). Resource-based theories of competitive advantage: A ten-year retrospective on the resource-based view. *Journal of Management, 27*(6), 643–650.

Barringer, B. R., & Harrison, J. S. (2000). Walking a tightrope: Creating value through interorganizational relationships. *Journal of Management, 26*(3), 367–403.

Beeby, M., & Booth, C. (2000). Networks and inter-organizational learning: A critical review. *The Learning Organization, 7*(2), 75–88.

Biermann, R., & Harsch, M. (2017). Resource dependence theory. In *Palgrave handbook of inter-organizational relations in world politics* (pp. 135–155). Palgrave Macmillan.

Bigliardi, B., Ferraro, G., Filippelli, S., & Galati, F. (2021). The past, present and future of open innovation. *European Journal of Innovation Management, 24*(4), 1130–1161.

Borgatti, S. P., & Foster, P. C. (2003). The network paradigm in organizational research: A review and typology. *Journal of Management, 29*(6), 991–1013.

Brass, D. J., Galaskiewicz, J., Greve, H. R., & Tsai, W. (2004). Taking stock of networks and organizations: A multilevel perspective. *Academy of Management Journal, 47*(6), 795–817.

Brusco, S. (1982). The Emilian model: Productive decentralisation and social integration. *Cambridge Journal of Economics, 6*(2), 167–184.

Carayannis, E. G., Grigoroudis, E., Campbell, D. F., Meissner, D., & Stamati, D. (2018). The ecosystem as helix: An exploratory theory-building study of regional co-opetitive entrepreneurial ecosystems as Quadruple/Quintuple Helix Innovation Models. *R&D Management, 48*(1), 148–162.

Carlsson, S. A. (2003). Knowledge managing and knowledge management systems in inter-organizational networks. *Knowledge and Process Management, 10*(3), 194–206.

Chesbrough, H. W. (2003). *Open innovation: The new imperative for creating and profiting from technology*. Harvard Business School.

Chesbrough, H. W., & Appleyard, M. M. (2007). Open innovation and strategy. *California Management Review, 50*(1), 57–76.

Christopher, M. (1992). *Logistics & supply chain management*. Pearson.

Coase, R. H. (1988). 1. The nature of the firm: Origin. *The Journal of Law, Economics, and Organization, 4*(1), 3–17.

Cooke, P., Uranga, M. G., & Etxebarria, G. (1998). Regional systems of innovation: An evolutionary perspective. *Environment and Planning A, 30*(9), 1563–1584.

Croom, S., Romano, P., & Giannakis, M. (2000). Supply chain management: An analytical framework for critical literature review. *European Journal of Purchasing & Supply Management, 6*(1), 67–83.

Das, T. K., & Rahman, N. (2010). Determinants of partner opportunism in strategic alliances: A conceptual framework. *Journal of Business and Psychology, 25*, 55–74.

Doloreux, D. (2002). What we should know about regional systems of innovation. *Technology in Society, 24*(3), 243–263.

Döring, T., & Schnellenbach, J. (2006). What do we know about geographical knowledge spillovers and regional growth?: A survey of the literature. *Regional Studies, 40*(03), 375–395.

Doz, Y. L. (1996). The evolution of cooperation in strategic alliances: Initial conditions or learning processes? *Strategic Management Journal, 17*(S1), 55–83.

Ebers, M. (1997). Explaining inter-organizational network formation. *The Formation of Inter-organizational Networks, 1*, 3–40.

Elmuti, D., & Kathawala, Y. (2001). An overview of strategic alliances. *Management Decision, 39*(3), 205–218.

Glaister, K. W., & Buckley, P. J. (1996). Strategic motives for international alliance formation. *Journal of Management Studies, 33*(3), 301–332.

Gomes-Casseres, B. (1997). Alliance strategies of small firms. *Small Business Economics, 9*(1), 33–44.

Grandori, A., & Soda, G. (1995). Inter-firm networks: Antecedents, mechanisms and forms. *Organization Studies, 16*(2), 183–214.

Granovetter, M. (1992). Economic institutions as social constructions: A framework for analysis. *Acta Sociologica, 35*(1), 3–11.

Gray, B. (1985). Conditions facilitating interorganizational collaboration. *Human Relations, 38*(10), 911–936.

Gulati, R., & Gargiulo, M. (1999). Where do interorganizational networks come from? *American Journal of Sociology, 104*(5), 1439–1493.

Hagedoorn, J. (1993). Strategic technology alliances and modes of cooperation in high-technology industries. In G. Grabher (Ed.), *The embedded firm: On the socioeconomics of industrial networks* (pp. 116–138). Routledge.

Hale, K. (2011). *How information matters: Networks and public policy innovation*. Georgetown University Press.

Hamel, G. (1991). Competition for competence and interpartner learning within international strategic alliances. *Strategic Management Journal, 12*(S1), 83–103.

Hamel, G., Doz, Y. L., & Prahalad, C. K. (1989). Collaborate with your competitors and win. *Harvard Business Review, 67*(1), 133–139.

Hergert, M., & Morris, D. (1988). Trends in international collaborative agreements. In F. Contractor & P. Lorange (Eds.), *Cooperative strategies in international business* (pp. 99–109). D.C. Heath.

Jaffe, A. B., Trajtenberg, M., & Henderson, R. (1993). Geographic localization of knowledge spillovers as evidenced by patent citations. *The Quarterly Journal of Economics, 108*(3), 577–598.

Keast, R., Mandell, M. P., Brown, K., & Woolcock, G. (2004). Network structures: Working differently and changing expectations. *Public Administration Review, 64*(3), 363–371.

Knight, L. (2002). Network learning: Exploring learning by interorganizational networks. *Human Relations, 55*(4), 427–454.

Knoke, D., & Yang, S. (2019). *Social network analysis*. Sage.

Lambert, D. M., Cooper, M. C., & Pagh, J. D. (1998). Supply chain management: Implementation issues and research opportunities. *The International Journal of Logistics Management, 9*(2), 1–20.

Larson, A. (1992). Network dyads in entrepreneurial settings: A study of the governance of exchange relationships. *Administrative Science Quarterly, 37*(1), 76–104.

Mariotti, S., & Cainarca, G. C. (1986). The evolution of transaction governance in the textile-clothing industry. *Journal of Economic Behaviour and Organization, 7*, 351–374.

McGuire, M. (2006). Collaborative public management: Assessing what we know and how we know it. *Public Administration Review, 66*, 33–43.

McLaren, T., Head, M., & Yuan, Y. (2002). Supply chain collaboration alternatives: Understanding the expected costs and benefits. *Internet Research, 12*(4), 348–364.

Milward, H. B., & Provan, K. G. (2006). *A manager's guide to choosing and using collaborative networks* (Vol. 8). IBM Center for the Business of Government.

Mowery, D. C. (Ed.). (1988). *International collaborative ventures in US manufacturing*. Ballinger.

Oliver, C. (1990). Determinants of interorganizational relationships: Integration and future directions. *Academy of Management Review, 15*(2), 241–265.

Penrose, E. T. (1959). *The theory of the growth of the firm*. Oxford University Press.

Pfeffer, J., & Salancik, G. (2015). External control of organizations—Resource dependence perspective. *Organizational Behavior, 2*, 355–370. Routledge.

Popp, J., MacKean, G. L., Casebeer, A., Milward, H. B., & Lindstrom, R. R. (2014). *Inter-organizational networks: A review of the literature to inform practice*. IBM Center for the Business of Government.

Porter, M. E. (2000). Location, competition, and economic development: Local clusters in a global economy. *Economic Development Quarterly, 14*(1), 15–34.

Powell, W. W. (1996). Inter-organizational collaboration in the biotechnology industry. *Journal of Institutional and Theoretical Economics (JITE)/Zeitschrift für die gesamte Staatswissenschaft*, 197–215.

Provan, K. G., Fish, A., & Sydow, J. (2007). Interorganizational networks at the network level: A review of the empirical literature on whole networks. *Journal of Management, 33*(3), 479–516.

Ring, P. S., & Van de Ven, A. H. (1994). Developmental processes of cooperative interorganizational relationships. *Academy of Management Review, 19*(1), 90–118.

Rossignoli, C., Ricciardi, F., Rossignoli, C., & Ricciardi, F. (2015). Theories explaining inter-organizational relationships in terms of coordination and control needs. In *Inter-organizational relationships: Towards a dynamic model for understanding business network performance* (pp. 7–36). Springer.

Scott, W. R. (2004). Institutional theory. *Encyclopedia of Social Theory, 11*, 408–414.
Sinton, L. J. (2020). *Service networks: A study of collaborative working in primary healthcare*. University of Liverpool.
Steers, R. M., Yoo, K. S., & Ungson, G. (1989). *The Chaebol: Korea's new industrial might*. Harper and Row.
Teece, D. J. (1986). Profiting from technological innovation: Implications for integration, collaboration, licensing and public policy. *Research Policy, 15*(6), 285–305.
Tidd, J., & Thuriaux-Alemán, B. (2016). Innovation management practices: Cross-sectorial adoption, variation, and effectiveness. *R&D Management, 46*(S3), 1024–1043.
Vargo, S. L., & Lusch, R. F. (2004). Evolving to a new dominant logic for marketing. *Journal of Marketing, 68*(1), 1–17.
Vargo, S. L., & Lusch, R. F. (2008a). From goods to service (s): Divergences and convergences of logics. *Industrial Marketing Management, 37*(3), 254–259.
Vargo, S. L., & Lusch, R. F. (2008b). Service-dominant logic: Continuing the evolution. *Journal of the Academy of Marketing Science, 36*, 1–10.
Vargo, S. L., & Lusch, R. F. (2014). Inversions of service-dominant logic. *Marketing Theory, 14*(3), 239–248.
Von Hippel, E. (1987). Cooperation between rivals: Informal know-how trading. *Research Policy, 16*(6), 291–302.
Westerlund, M., & Rajala, R. (2010). Learning and innovation in inter-organizational network collaboration. *Journal of Business & Industrial Marketing, 25*(6), 435–442.
Whipple, J. M., & Frankel, R. (2000). Strategic alliance success factors. *Journal of Supply Chain Management, 36*(2), 21–28.
Williamson, O. E. (1975). *Markets and hierarchies: Analysis and antitrust implications: A study in the economics of internal organization*. University of Illinois at Urbana-Champaign's Academy for Entrepreneurial Leadership Historical Research Reference in Entrepreneurship.
Williamson, O. E., & Winter, S. G. (Eds.). (1993). *The nature of the firm: Origins, evolution, and development*. Oxford University Press.
Zucker, L. G. (1987). Institutional theories of organization. *Annual Review of Sociology, 13*, 443–464.

Chapter 2
Artificial Intelligence and Its Role in the Healthcare Sector

Abstract This chapter explores the digitalisation phenomenon within the healthcare sector. Particularly, the author provides an overview of the transformative power of Artificial Intelligence (AI). Emphasis is placed on how this technology can maximise value in healthcare organisations and patient centricity.

The chapter concludes by addressing the transition from the concept of Industry 4.0 to Society 5.0, underlining the role of GenAI.

Particularly, the author explores its applications, benefits, and potential biases. Finally, the author investigates how GenAI can improve diagnoses and treatments, offering opportunities for more personalised and predictive healthcare.

Keywords Digitalisation · AI · GenAI · Service industry · Healthcare · Value creation

2.1 Evolution of Digitalisation in Healthcare

Despite the substantial body of knowledge collected over the past five decades, Digital Transformation (DT) has remained a prominent trend (Lanzolla et al., 2021). As Vial (2019) posits, the application of information, communication, and connectivity technologies enables DT to function as a *"process designed to improve an organisation by implementing significant changes in its characteristics"*. It has implications for many areas, including internal restructuring, digital asset acquisition, corporate operations, and the development of growth strategies. The introduction of complex technologies is a main consequence of DT, pushing companies to adapt their strategies to shifting consumer needs (Caputo et al., 2021). Among these technologies, AI plays a key role in boosting organisational efficiency.

It is described as the ability of computer-driven systems to perform activities that imitate human intelligence (Haenlein & Kaplan, 2019; Plastino & Purdy, 2018). It

A. Bastone, *The Power of Generative Artificial Intelligence for Value Co-Creation in Healthcare*, SpringerBriefs in Health Care Management and Economics, https://doi.org/10.1007/978-3-032-14298-6_2

has the potential to supplement or replace human labour in manufacturing, while software automation can manage routine administrative tasks such as scheduling. Similar in life sciences, including healthcare, using digital technologies has grown considerably (Leone et al., 2021).

The relevance of digital maturity in healthcare was underlined by the COVID-19 pandemic (Fletcher & Griffiths, 2020; Kraus et al., 2021). The necessity to preserve physical distance and guarantee continuity of care posed meaningful challenges. Improving patient flow within hospitals also became essential (Ting et al., 2020). Consequently, digital technologies should be viewed not merely as tools for improving specific activities but as catalysts for transforming relationships and processes both within organisations and across healthcare systems (Tighe et al., 2020). For example, data and geolocation technologies have supported bed management, treatment optimisation, and waiting list reduction, fostering innovative approaches to continuity of care (Anthony Jnr, 2021; Burrai et al., 2021).

In response to the post-pandemic imperatives of timeliness, safety, coordination, and patient value creation, the healthcare sector has undergone a paradigm shift (Giarelli & Vicarelli, 2021). As Porter (2010) emphasises, patient value should be the principal determinant of remuneration for healthcare actors. Value must be consistently defined around patient needs, with a patient-centred approach that prioritises outcomes over service volume.

Telemedicine, closely tied to healthcare's DT, has accelerated this shift. Ferorelli et al. (2020) define it as *"the delivery of healthcare services through information and communication technologies (ICT) in scenarios where healthcare professionals and patients are geographically separated"*. The increasing digital capability of healthcare workers has supported such advancements. Regularly updated clinical and organisational data, enabled by digital solutions, facilitate informed decision--making and timely information transfer (Prenestini & Marsilio, 2020).

Integrating AI into biological sciences has also become a dominant trend. Indeed, pharmaceutical companies adopt high-productivity screening to test several compounds on disease models simultaneously (Aldewachi et al., 2021). Specialised platforms supervise complex automated operations, while advanced robotics handle repetitive tasks. Each stage—from sample preparation and experimental design to data analysis—can be sustained by modular or fully integrated robotic systems. In medical devices, advanced technologies as intelligent catheters and autonomous surgical robots are compelling innovations (Peters et al., 2018). These advancements enhance outcomes in complex procedures and enable minimally invasive surgery. Particularly, in 2017, Stryker introduced the Mako robotic system for total knee arthroplasty, marking a significant step forward in this field (Van den Heuvel et al., 2018).

Despite its advantages, healthcare DT faces significant challenges. The sector's high level of regulation often slows innovation (Schiavone & Simoni, 2019). Complex regulatory frameworks contribute to coordination difficulties, reduced efficiency, and increased costs (Hansen & Baroody, 2020). Regulatory systems aim to protect population from risks such as unsafe drugs, epidemic outbreaks, harmful behaviours, and exposure to addictive substances (Mensa Sorato et al., 2020).

Another characteristic of the health sector is its resistance to change. Resistance is defined as *"any behaviour aimed at maintaining the status quo in the face of pressure to change it"* (Zaltman & Wallendorf, 1979) and often arises when individuals feel threatened (Ram, 1987). Employees may fear replacement by AI or resist incorporating it into daily practice (Huang & Rust, 2018). Although AI's predictive capabilities can surpass human performance in some contexts, enabling high-quality and personalised care (Agrawal et al., 2018), machines cannot make independent decisions. Thus, augmentation, emphasising a symbiotic relationship between humans and technology, is critical (Raisch & Krakowski, 2021).

A lack of digital expertise can also lead to resistance to AI solutions (Du et al., 2019; Li et al., 2023). Negative perceptions of technology's advantages further intensify resistance (Jebarajakirthy & Shankar, 2021). Additionally, privacy concerns and the automated treatment of sensitive data are still pressing questions (De Villiers et al., 2021). Furthermore, healthcare professionals need training to acquire the digital skills essential to integrate cutting-edge technologies (Kuek & Hakkennes, 2020). Thus, while AI has the potential to reform healthcare, its implementation depends on overcoming regulatory, technical, and human barriers. The following sections investigate these issues further, providing an exploration of the benefits and challenges of AI in healthcare.

2.2 Artificial Intelligence and Value-Creation in Healthcare

2.2.1 Artificial Intelligence and Sustainability

As Uzunidis (2009) asserts, sustainability is imperative for corporate growth and expansion. Indeed, businesses must consider the impact of their operations on both communities and the environment, in addition to the pursuit of financial objectives (Giret, 2019; Kayikci, 2018). Thus, sustainable development has been recognised as a fundamental element in determining an organisation's competitiveness (Sachs et al., 2019; Yang et al., 2022).

The World Commission on Environment and Development (1987) defined sustainable development as *"a model that is capable of meeting current needs without compromising the ability of future generations to meet their own needs"*. The triple-bottom-line (TBL) approach represents a validated theoretical framework, supporting firms to evaluate their impacts from social, environmental, and economic viewpoints in addition to the conventional revenue objective (Elkington, 1997). Integrating social, economic, and environmental considerations is essential for facilitating the implementation of strategies that yield long-term benefits for the environment, society, and the economy (Carter & Rogers, 2008; Tseng et al., 2020).

The notion of sustainability is acquiring increasing significance within the domain of health. As Yumnam (2024) argues, the specific goal of SDG target 3.8 is to *"achieve universal health coverage, ensuring financial risk protection, access to high-quality essential healthcare services, and safe, effective, and affordable essential medicines and vaccines"*. Thus, a *"One Health"* strategy is required (Bjørn et al., 2021), highlighting the interrelation of environmental, animal, and human health (https://www.iss.it/one-health).

Thus, the 2030 Agenda underlines the complex interconnection between social, economic, and cultural contexts and health (Sachs et al., 2019). Healthcare innovation must consider the dynamics of the system, as well as the socioeconomic structures in the area, to be deemed sustainable (Zollo et al., 2016).

The potential of AI to optimise resources and processes qualifies it as a crucial tool for advancing sustainability (Ilan, 2021; Tsagkaris et al., 2021). However, its implementation implies significant energy consumption. Therefore, healthcare organisations are identifying strategies for more sustainable adoption of it (Dhar, 2020). Indeed, developing inclusive and cooperative tactics supporting stakeholder well-being and advancing a long-term sustainability culture is essential for this to occur (Di Vaio et al., 2020; Eikelenboom & de Jong, 2019). This organisational culture has the potential to facilitate long-term economic sustainability and mitigate resistance to change.

A huge number of organisations employ integrated performance monitoring and control systems that evaluate economic, social, and ecological sustainability. These systems are designed to ensure the sustainable implementation of AI. It is imperative to ensure that the quality of care is both observable and quantifiable (Agrawal et al., 2019; Schiavone et al., 2022). This enables managers to strike a balance between control, growth, and economic goals while assisting them in accomplishing business objectives (Martins et al., 2020). Several studies highlighted the significant improvements in care quality and overall performance that result from the active evaluation process, which pays close attention to current practices and builds long-lasting partnerships (Bastone et al., 2024; Martins et al., 2020; Mikalef & Gupta, 2021; Schiavone et al., 2022).

2.2.2 Human Resource Management and Organisational Performance in the Era of AI

As extensively documented, the emergence of COVID-19 has precipitated a healthcare emergency, hindering the capacity of the healthcare ecosystem to enhance performance while upholding the standards of high-quality care, optimising human resource management, monitoring performance, and rationalising and allocating limited resources (Khalifa & Zabani, 2016; Li et al., 2023).

This concept may be further developed by healthcare institutions, which can utilise AI as a valuable tool for enhancing staff management (Frey & Osborne, 2017). Despite the centrality of human judgement in business operations, there has been a notable increase in the automation of these procedures, driven by the integration of advanced technologies such as AI. These technologies potentially reduce the time and expenses associated with hiring by ensuring efficient management and selection of qualified candidates (Woods et al., 2020).

To achieve maximum organisational performance, businesses must restructure HRM procedures, given that collaborative efforts and information sharing are essential to the joint adoption of digital technologies (Bouncken et al., 2021). As Gerards et al. (2021) have highlighted, this change incentivises workers to embrace intrapreneurial behaviours, ensuring they perform exceptionally well on their own and greatly enhancing the organisation's overall results.

The development of hybrid skills, the minimisation of repetitive tasks and the optimisation of resource sharing are but a few of the advantages of using digital technologies (Frey & Osborne, 2017; Neufeind et al., 2018; Tambe et al., 2019). As *"intelligent human resource management leads to greater economic growth"*, it can be posited that these advantages have a positive effect on an organisation's performance (Kumar et al., 2022).

As Hamilton and Sodeman (2020) and Paschen et al. (2020) argue, AI is a powerful predictive tool for determining customer demands and customising solutions. This is due to its capacity to process massive amounts of data. This capability is argued to ensure a competitive advantage and improve business performance by assisting human resources managers in selecting the most suitable candidates based on recruiters' expectations (Li et al., 2023). In the same context, the human resource's function is emphasised as both a unique asset and a source of competitive advantage (Amarakoon et al., 2018). Performance evaluations have the potential to serve as a catalyst for innovation and to align employee conduct with business objectives (Nijp et al., 2016; Yin & Qin, 2019). To capture the dynamism of an environment characterised by ongoing technological evolution, organisational changes, and procedural updates, it is necessary to reevaluate traditional performance measurement systems in the digital age (Kamble et al., 2020; Sahlin & Angelis, 2019; Schiavone et al., 2022; Yin & Qin, 2019).

According to Agrawal et al. (2019), two noteworthy aspects of effectiveness in the healthcare sector are identified. Firstly, increasing access to treatment, and secondly, enhancing the effectiveness of care delivery. The multifaceted nature of health care performance evaluation stems from the coordinated efforts of several organisations and individuals (Barbazza et al., 2021). The necessity of creating performance metrics that can capture this multidimensionality has been highlighted by this complexity (Schiavone et al., 2022).

By accelerating activities, reducing bottlenecks, and enhancing overall efficiency, AI systems can further facilitate performance analysis processes (Akter et al., 2020; Rana et al., 2022). Furthermore, by expanding access to data and insights that might otherwise be difficult to obtain, AI may facilitate better decision-making (Buçinca et al., 2021; Kumar et al., 2022). Indeed, sophisticated decision-support models can enhance decision-making processes and facilitate a deeper understanding of managerial dynamics (Martins et al., 2020). Additionally, AI is a powerful tool for enhancing healthcare functionality, effective staff knowledge management, resource optimisation, and elevating the quality of care, attributable to its advanced predictive capabilities (Yu et al., 2018).

2.2.3 AI's Impact on Organisational Competitive Position

As previously mentioned, it demonstrates how AI technology can give the healthcare sector a competitive advantage (Farahani et al., 2018; Fiaz et al., 2018). The digitalisation process has replaced a structure-focused approach to healthcare management with a patient- and team-focused one (Håkansson Eklund et al., 2019; Schiavone et al., 2022). Accordingly, AI can improve process quality, reduce healthcare costs, and increase accessibility to services, all of which will optimise patients' health experiences (Ali Mohamad et al., 2023; Appio et al., 2020; Leone et al., 2021; Teece, 2018).

Due to the phenomenon of global marketisation and the progressive integration of national economies into the global economy, modern technologies are essential, and processes and skills must adapt to preserve competitiveness (Ferreira et al., 2022; Ziyadin et al., 2018). Incorporating contemporary IT technologies into patient care services improves care quality in terms of diagnostic and treatment turnaround times (Hong & Lee, 2018). Implementing these IT systems generates new data to help healthcare professionals provide precise diagnoses and personalised treatment.

Thus, these technologies can guarantee healthcare facilities a competitive edge and impact a range of organisational operations and characteristics. As previously mentioned, AI systems significantly impact HRM processes. Specifically, they can improve talent acquisition (Johnson et al., 2020; Pillai & Sivathanu, 2020), maximise profits by providing decision support and automating employee tasks (Ivaschenko et al., 2021; Pereira et al., 2023) and enhance the performance of HR staff on tasks (Sturm et al., 2021).

Additionally, AI facilitates communication between various ecosystem participants, enabling healthcare organisations to implement a *"continuum of care"* (Leone et al., 2021). According to Agrawal et al. (2018), AI can be transferred across many areas, thereby increasing an organisation's competitiveness in a variety of markets. To reap the full benefits of AI, organisations must be able to adapt their business plans and strategies in response to changes in the external environment (Mathai et al., 2017). Implementing digital technology offers special talents and capacities (Rialti et al., 2019). Consequently, a firm's competitive position is impacted by acquiring new organisational and strategic competencies (Chakravorty et al., 2020).

2.2.4 Developing New Skills to Implement AI

The development of the digital skills required to adopt new technologies to their full potential is a frequently discussed issue in the context of digitisation (Kateryna et al., 2020). Industry 4.0 technologies require specific skills for effective use (Gliszczyński & Ciszewska-Mlinarič, 2021). Consequently, digitisation involves a thorough evolution of the value chain, with significant modifications of business models that adapt to digitalised systems (Parmentier & Mangematin, 2014; Vial, 2019).

The importance of employee training in enhancing digital literacy is emphasised (Cetindamar Kozanoglu & Abedin, 2021; Vial, 2019; Warner & Wäger, 2019). Digital literacy encompasses individuals' or social groups' capabilities when engaging with technology (Cetindamar Kozanoglu & Abedin, 2021). Higher digital literacy levels are associated with greater adoption of new technologies within organisations. Improved skills enable employees to identify opportunities offered by new technologies and investigate creative ways to utilise them (Gauthier et al., 2018; Vyas et al., 2017).

Nevertheless, embracing new technologies and developing one's abilities go hand in hand. As noted by the OECD (2022), *"the adoption of new digital technologies can improve the way people learn, where, when, and how they work, and stimulate their engagement in society by extending everyone's ability to collect, interpret, and analyse information and communicate with others around the world seamlessly"*. According to Van Laar et al. (2020), to successfully implement AI-based solutions, healthcare workers need to acquire both clinical and technological skills. As these skills directly impact patient safety and influence the likelihood of clinical and decision-making errors, their significance in the healthcare industry is clear (Kraus et al., 2021).

The integration of digital technology into healthcare should be accompanied by cultural changes that highlight the potential and advantages of such technologies (Laurenza et al., 2018). This culture must permeate the entire organisational structure (Verhoef et al., 2021). As previously mentioned, resistance to change is extremely strong in this industry, so inflexibility is a major obstacle to innovations (Chatterjee et al., 2022). As teams embrace change, digital technology becomes the primary tool for transforming organisations through the adoption of new technologies (Shah & Murthi, 2021).

2.2.5 The Role of AI in Managing Data

Data is essential to the operations of healthcare systems (Samuel & Lucassen, 2022; Yeng et al., 2021). Thus, healthcare systems produce a lot of information, necessitating effective methods to handle possible malfunctions. Industry 4.0 plays a revolutionary role by establishing guidelines for information management and improving operational effectiveness (Cannavale et al., 2022). The adoption of digital technology has made advanced techniques for gathering and processing enormous volumes of data possible (Flyverbom et al., 2019; Wang et al., 2021). While AI enables enhanced data processing, data analytics and Big Data tools are employed for management purposes. Technologies such as the Internet of Things (IoT) and cloud computing smoothen data collection and interaction across devices (Gupta et al., 2020; Marques & Ferreira, 2020).

Moreover, AI-based solutions allow for reduced medical errors, improved diagnosis and treatment effectiveness, and enhanced managerial and logistical processes (Lyon et al., 2021). Electronic medical records incorporate several information sources that are stored securely on cloud platforms. Initially stored on local servers, these documents are then made available over secure internet networks (Yang et al., 2019). This procedure guarantees reliable data processing and quality (Secinaro et al., 2021). Effective data utilisation has enormous potential to reduce costs, eliminate duplication, and greatly enhance service quality. Patients can often provide valuable data via wearable devices, health apps, and digital records (Kulkov et al., 2024; Pal et al., 2019). This allows for the rapid implementation of personalised interventions by enabling healthcare practitioners to monitor patients' health on a larger scale (Cafiero et al., 2023).

AI is also essential for increasing cost transparency, developing telemedicine, expanding access to treatment and reducing hospital visit duration and expenses. AI-powered digital medical records best demonstrate these advantages, improving diagnostic and clinical results by simplifying patient care and information management (Dash et al., 2019). AI can improve the effectiveness of social services and healthcare by helping to identify environmental and social barriers to health. Furthermore, AI is a vital tool for safeguarding sensitive data within healthcare systems against cyberattacks (Ansari et al., 2022).

Despite the high costs that characterise the shift to a value-based healthcare model, using AI is key in facilitating a faster and more efficient process. However, ethical, privacy, security, and regulatory issues result from managing healthcare data. It is essential to strike a balance between utilising new technology and safeguarding personal information (Mele et al., 2023; Russo-Spena et al., 2022).

Obstacles to implementing AI in healthcare data management include older systems, cybersecurity flaws, and privacy issues. This is more evident in highly regulated sectors, where strict regulations and compliance costs often hinder the adoption of new technologies (Schiavone & Simoni, 2019). This resistance to change results in inefficiencies, as data cannot be used or analysed. Furthermore, while gathering and processing private information is necessary for creating new services, there is a risk of misuse or unauthorised disclosure, which could harm individuals (Mele et al., 2023).

Government organisations play a key role in striking a balance between innovation and social welfare. However, growing regulatory limitations make the deployment of AI technologies more difficult. Existing research emphasises the need to balance protecting privacy with promoting innovation (Jarvenpaa & Wernick, 2011; Quach et al., 2022). This challenge remains one of the most important concerns for the future of the healthcare industry (Bastone et al., 2023).

2.2.6 *Artificial Intelligence as a Tool to Support Decision-Making*

As mentioned in the previous paragraphs, AI typically plays a significant role in organisations' decision-making processes (Agrawal et al., 2018). Due to the emergence of increasingly sophisticated innovations, businesses now must make judgements in chaotic and disorderly organisational contexts (Ganter & Hecker, 2013; Makowski & Kajikawa, 2021). From this perspective, AI offers automation, sophisticated analytics, and predictive capabilities, making it an effective tool for navigating this complexity (Kakatkar et al., 2020; Makowski & Kajikawa, 2021). Notably, AI systems can either support or replace human decision-makers (Edwards et al., 2000). Literature describes the great operational and tactical effectiveness of AI systems by saving time and money in this situation. Despite that, there is a lack of comprehension and creativity required for long-term, organised decision-making (Simon, 1987). From a decision-support standpoint, AI can offer recommendations to improve decision-making processes. However, the effectiveness of these tools depends heavily on user participation, so using them may not always reduce decision-making time.

In contrast to the early studies on AI applied to decision-making (Gorry & Scott Morton, 1971), technological advances have enhanced the capabilities of AI by qualifying it as a tool that can *"automate cognitive processes, provide insights through data analysis, and improve engagement with users and customers"* (Davenport & Ronanki, 2018). Through a thorough literature review, Pietronudo et al. (2022) highlight four key benefits of AI-assisted decision-making. (1) Augmented creativity: AI-based systems act as knowledge-creation accelerators, improving each individual's learning capabilities; (2) Renewed organisation: The use of AI affects the innovation process, creating a virtuous circle where innovation feeds innovation; (3) Renewed chaos: AI is not without its dark side, as the lack of rules governing its use raises issues of privacy, bias, and human control. (4) Augmented rationality: AI speeds up and optimises decision-making through improved data processing, enabling organisations to identify threats and opportunities early on. Even though AI speeds up and improves decision-making (Jarrahi, 2018; Lindebaum et al., 2020; Mahroof, 2019), there are several questions regarding how to successfully combine AI and humans' skills in terms of collaboration and synergy. Furthermore, as will be discussed in the following paragraphs, to guarantee the fairness and transparency of AI outcomes, algorithms that can identify possible biases must be created (Shrestha et al., 2019). This presents difficulties for managers, who must learn new skills to control input algorithms and interpret outcomes. Moreover, AI is rapidly evolving into increasingly complex systems that require continuous operational monitoring (Shrestha et al., 2019).

2.3 The Role of Generative Artificial Intelligence in Shifting from Industry 4.0 to Society 5.0

2.3.1 Applications, Benefits, and Biases of Generative Artificial Intelligence: A Focus on Healthcare

The Fourth Industrial Revolution led to useful systems for automating processes through sophisticated technologies (Schwab, 2017). These innovations shaped a connected, data-driven industrial ecosystem (Caputo et al., 2021). However, full automation fosters ethical and social concerns, such as the substitution of human labour (Huang & Rust, 2018). Thus, a new paradigm, the so-called Industry 5.0, has emerged, promoting a human-centred, sustainable, and resilient industrial context (Leng et al., 2022). Thus, it strengthens collaboration between people and machines, enabling more personalised and sustainable processes (Rani et al., 2024).

In this context, GenAI—based on systems able to produce original content autonomously—emerged (Clune, 2019).

As a driver of organisational change, GenAI automates complex and repetitive activities, increasing productivity (Hessari et al., 2024). It also enhances human–machine collaboration, reshaping industries and boosting profitability (Simkute et al., 2024). In logistics, GenAI streamlines data distribution and supplier management (Khlie et al., 2024). In e-commerce, GenAI-powered chatbots have transformed customer service, while in fashion, it supports virtual modelling and personalised design (Shaikh, 2023). In pharmaceuticals, it accelerates drug discovery and development, reducing costs and enabling tailored solutions (Doron et al., 2023). The benefits of these applications lie in reduced costs and time, improved customisation through predictive algorithms, and advanced data processing that supports real-time decision-making (Fosso Wamba et al., 2024).

Despite its promise, integrating GenAI into Industry 5.0 comes with challenges. Biased datasets can compromise reliability, reinforce stereotypes, and spread misinformation (O'Neil, 2017). High costs, resource demands, privacy concerns, and ethical issues further complicate adoption (Russo-Spena et al., 2022). Human oversight remains essential, since AI systems cannot yet navigate moral or ethical choices independently (McKendrick & Thurai, 2022). Bias in GenAI arises from unrepresentative data, embedded assumptions within algorithms, and user interactions that perpetuate prejudice (Ferrara, 2023). Such biases risk exacerbating inequalities, especially for marginalised groups, raising important questions about accountability and transparency (Azaria et al., 2024; Sedaghat, 2024). Addressing these risks requires systems that are transparent, adaptable, and user-controlled (Taherizadeh et al., 2018).

Healthcare is one of the sectors most affected by GenAI. It enables improved diagnostics, personalised medicine, and efficient medical writing. For instance, IBM Watson was developed to assist oncologists by synthesising clinical knowledge to suggest treatment options.

In drug development, its ability to generate and evaluate molecular structures in silico shortens discovery cycles and lowers costs, as demonstrated by AI-driven vaccines at Flinders University and R&D applications by Novartis and Roche (Doron et al., 2023; Harrer et al., 2024). These capabilities extend into personalised medicine, where access to large-scale genetic and clinical datasets allows for tailored treatments that minimise adverse effects and improve patient outcomes (Yim et al., 2024; Zhang & Kamel Boulos, 2023).

Wearable technologies powered by GenAI contribute to continuous patient monitoring by detecting early signs of conditions such as hypertension or diabetes (Leone et al., 2021). Sophisticated algorithms enable real-time tracking of vital indicators, facilitating early intervention and enhancing patient engagement (Nova, 2023).

Nevertheless, significant challenges persist. The variability and volume of healthcare data can compromise algorithmic effectiveness, especially when datasets lack diversity and fail to address disparities across populations (Ghassemi & Nsoesie, 2022). Data privacy and security are also pressing concerns, as violations could undermine trust and patients' rights (Kumar et al., 2024). Finally, overreliance on GenAI risks diminishing professional autonomy, potentially weakening clinical judgement (Solaiman & Cohen, 2024). For this reason, technology in healthcare should serve as a complement to human expertise, fostering balanced collaboration between humans and machines in the spirit of Industry 5.0.

References

Agrawal, A., Gans, J., & Goldfarb, A. (2018). Prediction, judgment, and complexity: A theory of decision-making and artificial intelligence. In *The economics of artificial intelligence: An agenda* (pp. 89–110). University of Chicago Press.

Agrawal, A., Gans, J. S., & Goldfarb, A. (2019). Exploring the impact of artificial intelligence: Prediction versus judgment. *Information Economics and Policy, 47*, 1–6.

Akter, S., Michael, K., Uddin, M. R., McCarthy, G., & Rahman, M. (2020). Transforming business using digital innovations: The application of AI, blockchain, cloud and data analytics. *Annals of Operations Research*, 1–33.

Aldewachi, H., Al-Zidan, R. N., Conner, M. T., & Salman, M. M. (2021). High-throughput screening platforms in the discovery of novel drugs for neurodegenerative diseases. *Bioengineering, 8*(2), 30.

Ali Mohamad, T., Bastone, A., Bernhard, F., & Schiavone, F. (2023). How artificial intelligence impacts the competitive position of healthcare organizations. *Journal of Organizational Change Management, 36*(8), 49–70.

Amarakoon, U., Weerawardena, J., & Verreynne, M. L. (2018). Learning capabilities, human resource management innovation and competitive advantage. *The International Journal of Human Resource Management, 29*(10), 1736–1766.

Ansari, M. F., Dash, B., Sharma, P., & Yathiraju, N. (2022). The impact and limitations of artificial intelligence in cybersecurity: A literature review. *International Journal of Advanced Research in Computer and Communication Engineering, 11*(9), 81–90.

Anthony Jnr, B. (2021). Integrating telemedicine to support digital health care for the management of COVID-19 pandemic. *International Journal of Healthcare Management, 14*(1), 280–289.

Appio, F. P., Frattini, F., Messeni Petruzzelli, A., & Neirotti, P. (2020). Digital transformation and innovation management: opening up the black box. *Journal of Product Innovation Management*, 1–6.
Azaria, A., Azoulay, R., & Reches, S. (2024). ChatGPT is a remarkable tool—For experts. *Data Intelligence, 6*(1), 240–296.
Barbazza, E., Klazinga, N. S., & Kringos, D. S. (2021). Exploring the actionability of healthcare performance indicators for quality of care: A qualitative analysis of the literature, expert opinion and user experience. *BMJ Quality & Safety, 30*(12), 1010–1020.
Bastone, A., Nevi, G., Schiavone, F., Bernhard, F., & Dezi, L. (2024). Making artificial intelligence sustainable for healthcare. *Journal of Innovation Economics & Management, 44*(2), 87–117.
Bastone, A., Schiavone, F., Carli, M. R., & Juárez-Varón, D. (2023). How to shorten the market entry innovation in a highly regulated market. The case of early access programs in the pharmaceutical industry. *International Entrepreneurship and Management Journal, 19*(4), 1561–1581.
Bjørn, P., Wulff, M., Petræus, M. S., & Møller, N. H. (2021). Immersive cooperative work environments (CWE): Designing human-building interaction in virtual reality. *Computer Supported Cooperative Work (CSCW), 30*(3), 351–391.
Bouncken, R. B., Kraus, S., & Roig-Tierno, N. (2021). Knowledge-and innovation-based business models for future growth: Digitalized business models and portfolio considerations. *Review of Managerial Science, 15*(1), 1–14.
Buçinca, Z., Malaya, M. B., & Gajos, K. Z. (2021). To trust or to think: Cognitive forcing functions can reduce overreliance on AI in AI-assisted decision-making. *Proceedings of the ACM on Human-Computer Interaction, 5*(CSCW1), 1–21.
Burrai, F., Micheluzzi, V., & Apuzzo, L. (2021). Governance nell'innovazione: Sanità Digitale, mobile health, big data, virtual reality. *Giornale di Clinica Nefrologica e Dialisi, 33*(1), 42–50.
Cafiero, G., De Rosa, M., & Schiavone, F. (2023). Improving healthcare by designing AI-human-centered systems. In F. P. Appio, D. La Torre, F. Lazzeri, H. Masri, & F. Schiavone (Eds.), *Impact of artificial intelligence in business and society* (pp. 250–269). Routledge.
Cannavale, C., Esempio Tammaro, A., Leone, D., & Schiavone, F. (2022). Innovation adoption in inter-organizational healthcare networks—The role of artificial intelligence. *European Journal of Innovation Management, 25*(6), 758–774.
Caputo, A., Pizzi, S., Pellegrini, M. M., & Dabić, M. (2021). Digitalisation and business models: Where are we going? A science map of the field. *Journal of Business Research, 123*, 489–501.
Carter, C. R., & Rogers, D. S. (2008). A framework of sustainable supply chain management: Moving toward new theory. *International Journal of Physical Distribution & Logistics Management, 38*(5), 360–387.
Cetindamar Kozanoglu, D., & Abedin, B. (2021). Understanding the role of employees in digital transformation: Conceptualization of digital literacy of employees as a multi-dimensional organizational affordance. *Journal of Enterprise Information Management, 34*(6), 1649–1672.
Chakravorty, T., Jha, K., Barthwal, S., & Chakraborty, S. (2020). Digital technologies as antecedents to process integration and dynamic capabilities in healthcare: An empirical investigation. *Journal of International Technology and Information Management, 28*(4), 84–111.
Chatterjee, S., Chaudhuri, R., & Vrontis, D. (2022). Does remote work flexibility enhance organization performance? Moderating role of organization policy and top management support. *Journal of Business Research, 139*, 1501–1512.
Clune, J. (2019). AI-GAs: AI-generating algorithms, an alternate paradigm for producing general artificial intelligence. *arXiv Preprint*. https://doi.org/10.48550/arXiv.1905.10985
Dash, S., Shakyawar, S. K., Sharma, M., & Kaushik, S. (2019). Big data in healthcare: Management, analysis and future prospects. *Journal of Big Data, 6*(1), 1–25.
Davenport, T. H., & Ronanki, R. (2018). Artificial intelligence for the real world. *Harvard Business Review, 96*(1), 108–116.
De Villiers, C., Kuruppu, S., & Dissanayake, D. (2021). A (new) role for business—Promoting the United Nations' Sustainable Development Goals through the internet-of-things and blockchain technology. *Journal of Business Research, 131*, 598–609.

Dhar, P. (2020). The carbon impact of artificial intelligence. *Nature Machine Intelligence, 2*(8), 423–425.

Di Vaio, A., Palladino, R., Hassan, R., & Escobar, O. (2020). Artificial intelligence and business models in the sustainable development goals perspective: A systematic literature review. *Journal of Business Research, 121*, 283–314.

Doron, G., Genway, S., Roberts, M., & Jasti, S. (2023). New horizons: Pioneering pharmaceutical R&D with generative AI from lab to the clinic—An industry perspective. *arXiv Preprint*. https://doi.org/10.48550/arXiv.2312.12482

Du, W. D., Pan, S. L., Leidner, D. E., & Ying, W. (2019). Affordances, experimentation and actualization of FinTech: A blockchain implementation study. *The Journal of Strategic Information Systems, 28*(1).

Edwards, J. S., Duan, Y., & Robins, P. C. (2000). An analysis of expert systems for business decision making at different levels and in different roles. *European Journal of Information Systems, 9*(1), 36–46.

Eikelenboom, M., & de Jong, G. (2019). The impact of dynamic capabilities on the sustainability performance of SMEs. *Journal of Cleaner Production, 235*, 1360–1370.

Elkington, J. (1997). *The triple bottom line of 21st century business*. Capstone.

Farahani, B., Firouzi, F., Chang, V., Badaroglu, M., Constant, N., & Mankodiya, K. (2018). Towards fog-driven IoT eHealth: Promises and challenges of IoT in medicine and healthcare. *Future Generation Computer Systems, 78*, 659–676.

Ferorelli, D., Nardelli, L., Spagnolo, L., Corradi, S., Silvestre, M., Misceo, F., & Dell'Erba, A. (2020). Medical legal aspects of telemedicine in Italy: Application fields, professional liability and focus on care services during the COVID-19 health emergency. *Journal of Primary Care & Community Health, 11*, 2150132720985055.

Ferrara, E. (2023). *Should chatgpt be biased? Challenges and risks of bias in large language models*. arXiv preprint arXiv:2304.03738.

Ferreira, J. J., Veiga, P. M., Fernandes, C. I., & Kraus, S. (2022). B2B marketing strategies in healthcare management: Intellectual structure and research trends. *Journal of Business & Industrial Marketing, 37*(8), 1580–1593.

Fiaz, M., Ikram, A., & Ilyas, A. (2018). Enterprise resource planning systems: Digitisation of healthcare service quality. *Administrative Sciences, 8*(3), 38.

Fletcher, G., & Griffiths, M. (2020). Digital transformation during a lockdown. *International Journal of Information Management, 55*, 102185.

Flyverbom, M., Deibert, R., & Matten, D. (2019). The governance of digital technology, big data, and the internet: New roles and responsibilities for business. *Business & Society, 58*(1), 3–19.

Fosso Wamba, S., Guthrie, C., Queiroz, M. M., & Minner, S. (2024). ChatGPT and generative artificial intelligence: An exploratory study of key benefits and challenges in operations and supply chain management. *International Journal of Production Research, 62*(16), 5676–5696.

Frey, C. B., & Osborne, M. A. (2017). The future of employment: How susceptible are jobs to computerisation? *Technological Forecasting and Social Change, 114*, 254–280.

Ganter, A., & Hecker, A. (2013). Deciphering antecedents of organizational innovation. *Journal of Business Research, 66*(5), 575–584.

Gauthier, C., Bastianutti, J., & Haggège, M. (2018). Managerial capabilities to address digital business models: The case of digital health. *Strategic Change, 27*(2), 173–180.

Gerards, R., van Wetten, S., & van Sambeek, C. (2021). New ways of working and intrapreneurial behaviour: The mediating role of transformational leadership and social interaction. *Review of Managerial Science, 15*(7), 2075–2110.

Ghassemi, M., & Nsoesie, E. O. (2022). In medicine, how do we machine learn anything real? *Patterns, 3*(1).

Giarelli, G., & Vicarelli, G. (2021). *Libro Bianco Il Servizio Sanitario Nazionale e la pandemia da Covid-19: Problemi e proposte* (pp. 1–146). Franco Angeli.

Giret, A. (2019). Smart and sustainable urban logistic applications aided by intelligent techniques. *Service Oriented Computing and Applications, 13*(3), 185–186.

Gliszczyński, M., & Ciszewska-Mlinarič, M. (2021). Digital twin and medical devices: Technological significance of convergent inventions. *Journal of Global Information Technology Management, 24*(2), 134–148.

Gorry, G. A., & Scott Morton, M. S. (1971). A framework for management information systems. *Sloan Management Review, 13*.

Gupta, S., Leszkiewicz, A., Kumar, V., Bijmolt, T., & Potapov, D. (2020). Digital analytics: Modeling for insights and new methods. *Journal of Interactive Marketing, 51*(1), 26–43.

Haenlein, M., & Kaplan, A. (2019). A brief history of artificial intelligence: On the past, present, and future of artificial intelligence. *California Management Review, 61*(4), 5–14.

Håkansson Eklund, J., Holmström, I. K., Kumlin, T., Kaminsky, E., Skoglund, K., Höglander, J., Sundler, A. J., Condén, E., & Summer Merenius, M. (2019). Same same or different? A review of reviews of person-centred and patient-centred care. *Patient Education and Counselling, 102*(1), 3–11.

Hamilton, R. H., & Sodeman, W. A. (2020). The questions we ask: Opportunities and challenges for using big data analytics to strategically manage human capital resources. *Business Horizons, 63*(1), 85–95.

Hansen, S., & Baroody, A. J. (2020). Electronic health records and the logics of care: Complementarity and conflict in the US healthcare system. *Information Systems Research, 31*(1), 57–75.

Harrer, S., Menard, J., Rivers, M., Green, D. V., Karpiak, J., Jeliazkov, J. R., Shapovalov, M. V., del Alamo, D., & Sternke, M. C. (2024). Artificial intelligence drives the digital transformation of pharma. In C. Krittanawong (Ed.), *Artificial intelligence in clinical practice* (pp. 345–372). Academic Press.

Hessari, H., Bai, A., & Daneshmandi, F. (2024). Generative AI: Boosting adaptability and reducing workplace overload. *Journal of Computer Information Systems*, 1–14.

Hong, K. S., & Lee, D. (2018). Impact of operational innovations on customer loyalty in the healthcare sector. *Service Business, 12*(3), 575–600.

Huang, M. H., & Rust, R. T. (2018). Artificial intelligence in service. *Journal of Service Research, 21*(2), 155–172.

Ilan, Y. (2021). Improving global healthcare and reducing costs using second-generation artificial intelligence-based digital pills: A market disruptor. *International Journal of Environmental Research and Public Health, 18*(2), 811.

Ivaschenko, A., Diyazitdinova, A. R., & Nikiforova, T. (2021). Optimisation of the rational proportion of intelligent technologies application in service organisations. *Organizacija, 54*(2), 162–177.

Jarrahi, M. H. (2018). Artificial intelligence and the future of work: Human-AI symbiosis in organizational decision making. *Business Horizons, 61*(4), 577–586.

Jarvenpaa, S. L., & Wernick, A. (2011). Paradoxical tensions in open innovation networks. *European Journal of Innovation Management, 14*(4), 521–548.

Jebarajakirthy, C., & Shankar, A. (2021). Impact of online convenience on mobile banking adoption intention: A moderated mediation approach. *Journal of Retailing and Consumer Services, 58*, 102323.

Johnson, R. D., Stone, D. L., & Lukaszewski, K. M. (2020). The benefits of eHRM and AI for talent acquisition. *Journal of Tourism Futures, 7*(1), 40–52.

Kakatkar, C., Bilgram, V., & Füller, J. (2020). Innovation analytics: Leveraging artificial intelligence in the innovation process. *Business Horizons, 63*(2), 171–181.

Kamble, S. S., Gunasekaran, A., Ghadge, A., & Raut, R. (2020). A performance measurement system for industry 4.0 enabled smart manufacturing system in SMMEs—A review and empirical investigation. *International Journal of Production Economics, 229*, 107853.

Kateryna, A., Oleksandr, R., Mariia, T., Iryna, S., Evgen, K., & Anastasiia, L. (2020). Digital literacy development trends in the professional environment. *International Journal of Learning, Teaching and Educational Research, 19*(7), 55–79.

Kayikci, Y. (2018). Sustainability impact of digitization in logistics. *Procedia Manufacturing, 21*, 782–789.

Khalifa, M., & Zabani, I. (2016). Utilizing health analytics in improving the performance of healthcare services: A case study on a tertiary care hospital. *Journal of Infection and Public Health, 9*(6), 757–765.

Khlie, K., Benmamoun, Z., Jebbor, I., & Serrou, D. (2024). Generative AI for enhanced operations and supply chain management. *Journal of Infrastructure, Policy and Development, 8*(10), 6637.

Kraus, S., Schiavone, F., Pluzhnikova, A., & Invernizzi, A. C. (2021). Digital transformation in healthcare: Analyzing the current state-of-research. *Journal of Business Research, 123*, 557–567.

Kuek, A., & Hakkennes, S. (2020). Healthcare staff digital literacy levels and their attitudes towards information systems. *Health Informatics Journal, 26*(1), 592–612.

Kulkov, I., Kulkova, J., Leone, D., Rohrbeck, R., & Menvielle, L. (2024). Stand-alone or run together: Artificial intelligence as an enabler for other technologies. *International Journal of Entrepreneurial Behavior & Research, 30*(8), 2082–2105.

Kumar, D., Dhalwal, R., & Chaudhary, A. (2024). Exploring the ethical implications of generative AI in healthcare. In R. Kumar, A. Joshi, & H. O. Sharan (Eds.), *The ethical frontier of AI and data analysis* (pp. 180–195). IGI Global.

Kumar, M., Raut, R. D., Mangla, S. K., Ferraris, A., & Choubey, V. K. (2022). The adoption of artificial intelligence powered workforce management for effective revenue growth of micro, small, and medium scale enterprises (MSMEs). *Production Planning & Control*, 1–17.

Lanzolla, G., Pesce, D., & Tucci, C. L. (2021). The digital transformation of search and recombination in the innovation function: Tensions and an integrative framework. *Journal of Product Innovation Management, 38*(1), 90–113.

Laurenza, E., Quintano, M., Schiavone, F., & Vrontis, D. (2018). The effect of digital technologies adoption in healthcare industry: A case based analysis. *Business Process Management Journal, 24*(5), 1124–1144.

Leng, J., Sha, W., Wang, B., Zheng, P., Zhuang, C., Liu, Q., Wuest, T., Mourtzis, D., & Wang, L. (2022). Industry 5.0: Prospect and retrospect. *Journal of Manufacturing Systems, 65*, 279–295.

Leone, D., Schiavone, F., Appio, F. P., & Chiao, B. (2021). How does artificial intelligence enable and enhance value co-creation in industrial markets? An exploratory case study in the healthcare ecosystem. *Journal of Business Research, 129*, 849–859.

Li, P., Bastone, A., Mohamad, T. A., & Schiavone, F. (2023). How does artificial intelligence impact human resources performance. evidence from a healthcare institution in the United Arab Emirates. *Journal of Innovation & Knowledge, 8*(2), 100340.

Lindebaum, D., Vesa, M., & Den Hond, F. (2020). Insights from "the machine stops" to better understand rational assumptions in algorithmic decision making and its implications for organizations. *Academy of Management Review, 45*(1), 247–263.

Lyon, J. Y., Bogodistov, Y., & Moormann, J. (2021). AI-driven optimization in healthcare: The diagnostic process. *European Journal of Management Issues, 29*(4), 218–231.

Mahroof, K. (2019). A human-centric perspective exploring the readiness towards smart warehousing: The case of a large retail distribution warehouse. *International Journal of Information Management, 45*, 176–190.

Makowski, P. T., & Kajikawa, Y. (2021). automation-driven innovation management? Toward innovation-automation-strategy cycle. *Technological Forecasting and Social Change, 168*, 120723.

Marques, I. C., & Ferreira, J. J. (2020). Digital transformation in the area of health: Systematic review of 45 years of evolution. *Health and Technology, 10*(3), 575–586.

Martins, S. M., Ferreira, F. A., Ferreira, J. J., & Marques, C. S. (2020). An artificial-intelligence-based method for assessing service quality: Insights from the prosthodontics sector. *Journal of Service Management, 31*(2), 291–312.

Mathai, N., Shiratudin, M. F., & Sohel, F. (2017). Electronic health record management: Expectations, issues, and challenges. *Journal of Health & Medical Informatics, 8*(3), 1–5.

McKendrick, J., & Thurai, A. (2022). AI isn't ready to make unsupervised decisions. *Harvard Business Review, 15*, 10.

Mele, C., Spena, T. R., Marzullo, M., & Di Bernardo, I. (2023). The phygital transformation: A systematic review and a research agenda. *Italian Journal of Marketing, 2023*(3), 323–349.

Mensa Sorato, M., Davari, M., Abdollahi Asl, A., Soleymani, F., & Kebriaeezadeh, A. (2020). Why healthcare market needs government intervention to improve access to essential medicines and healthcare efficiency: A scoping review from pharmaceutical price regulation perspective. *Journal of Pharmaceutical Health Services Research, 11*(4), 321–333.

Mikalef, P., & Gupta, M. (2021). Artificial intelligence capability: Conceptualization, measurement calibration, and empirical study on its impact on organizational creativity and firm performance. *Information & Management, 58*(3), 103434.

Neufeind, M., O'Reilly, J., & Ranft, F. (Eds.). (2018). *Work in the digital age: Challenges of the fourth industrial revolution*. Rowman and Littlefield.

Nijp, H. H., Beckers, D. G., van de Voorde, K., Geurts, S. A., & Kompier, M. A. (2016). Effects of new ways of working on work hours and work location, health and job-related outcomes. *Chronobiology International, 33*(6), 604–618.

Nova, K. (2023). Generative AI in healthcare: Advancements in electronic health records, facilitating medical languages, and personalized patient care. *Journal of Advanced Analytics in Healthcare Management, 7*(1), 115–131.

OECD. (2022). *Skills for the digital transition: Assessing recent trends using big data*. OECD. https://doi.org/10.1787/38c36777-en

O'Neil, C. (2017). *Weapons of math destruction: How big data increases inequality and threatens democracy*. Crown.

Pal, D., Vanijja, V., Arpnikanondt, C., Zhang, X., & Papasratorn, B. (2019). A quantitative approach for evaluating the quality of experience of smart-wearables from the quality of data and quality of information: An end user perspective. *IEEE Access, 7*, 64266–64278.

Parmentier, G., & Mangematin, V. (2014). Orchestrating innovation with user communities in the creative industries. *Technological Forecasting and Social Change, 83*, 40–53.

Paschen, J., Wilson, M., & Ferreira, J. J. (2020). Collaborative intelligence: How human and artificial intelligence create value along the B2B sales funnel. *Business Horizons, 63*(3), 403–414.

Pereira, V., Hadjielias, E., Christofi, M., & Vrontis, D. (2023). A systematic literature review on the impact of artificial intelligence on workplace outcomes: A multi-process perspective. *Human Resource Management Review, 33*(1), 100857.

Peters, B. S., Armijo, P. R., Krause, C., Choudhury, S. A., & Oleynikov, D. (2018). Review of emerging surgical robotic technology. *Surgical Endoscopy, 32*, 1636–1655.

Pietronudo, M. C., Croidieu, G., & Schiavone, F. (2022). A solution looking for problems? A systematic literature review of the rationalizing influence of artificial intelligence on decision-making in innovation management. *Technological Forecasting and Social Change, 182*, 121828.

Pillai, R., & Sivathanu, B. (2020). Adoption of artificial intelligence (AI) for talent acquisition in IT/ITeS organizations. *Benchmarking: An International Journal, 27*(9), 2599–2629.

Plastino, E., & Purdy, M. (2018). Game changing value from Artificial Intelligence: Eight strategies. *Strategy & Leadership, 46*(1), 16–22.

Porter, M. E. (2010). What is value in health care? *New England Journal of Medicine, 363*(26), 2477–2481.

Prenestini, A., & Marsilio, M. (2020). La gestione delle operations in tempo di crisi: le prime 10 lezioni apprese dalle Aziende Sanitarie. *MECOSAN*, 155–164.

Quach, S., Thaichon, P., Martin, K. D., Weaven, S., & Palmatier, R. W. (2022). Digital technologies: Tensions in privacy and data. *Journal of the Academy of Marketing Science, 50*(6), 1299–1323.

Raisch, S., & Krakowski, S. (2021). Artificial intelligence and management: The automation–augmentation paradox. *Academy of Management Review, 46*(1), 192–210.

Ram, S. (1987). A model of innovation resistance. *Advances in Consumer Research, 14*.

Rana, N. P., Chatterjee, S., Dwivedi, Y. K., & Akter, S. (2022). Understanding dark side of artificial intelligence (AI) integrated business analytics: Assessing firm's operational inefficiency and competitiveness. *European Journal of Information Systems, 31*(3), 364–387.

Rani, S., Jining, D., Shoukat, K., Shoukat, M. U., & Nawaz, S. A. (2024). A human–machine interaction mechanism: Additive manufacturing for Industry 5.0—Design and management. *Sustainability, 16*(10), 4158.

Rialti, R., Marzi, G., Ciappei, C., & Busso, D. (2019). Big data and dynamic capabilities: A bibliometric analysis and systematic literature review. *Management Decision, 57*(2).

Russo-Spena, T., Mele, C., Cavacece, Y., Ebraico, S., Dantas, C., Roseiro, P., & van Staalduinen, W. (2022). Enabling value co-creation in healthcare through blockchain technology. *International Journal of Environmental Research and Public Health, 20*(1), 67.

Sachs, J. D., Schmidt-Traub, G., Mazzucato, M., Messner, D., Nakicenovic, N., & Rockström, J. (2019). Six transformations to achieve the sustainable development goals. *Nature Sustainability, 2*(9), 805–814.

Sahlin, J., & Angelis, J. (2019). Performance management systems: Reviewing the rise of dynamics and digitalization. *Cogent Business & Management, 6*(1), 1642293.

Samuel, G., & Lucassen, A. M. (2022). The environmental sustainability of data-driven health research: A scoping review. *Digital Health, 8*, 20552076221111297.

Schiavone, F., Leone, D., Caporuscio, A., & Kumar, A. (2022). Revealing the role of intellectual capital in digitalized health networks. A meso level analysis for building and monitoring a KPI dashboard. *Technological Forecasting and Social Change, 175*, 121325.

Schiavone, F., & Simoni, M. (2019). Strategic marketing approaches for the diffusion of innovation in highly regulated industrial markets: The value of market access. *Journal of Business & Industrial Marketing, 34*(7), 1606–1618.

Schwab, K. (2017). *The fourth industrial revolution*. Crown Currency.

Secinaro, S., Calandra, D., Secinaro, A., Muthurangu, V., & Biancone, P. (2021). The role of artificial intelligence in healthcare: A structured literature review. *BMC Medical Informatics and Decision Making, 21*, 1–23.

Sedaghat, S. (2024). Plagiarism and wrong content as potential challenges of using chatbots like ChatGPT in medical research. *Journal of Academic Ethics, 23*, 185–188.

Shah, D., & Murthi, B. P. S. (2021). Marketing in a data-driven digital world: Implications for the role and scope of marketing. *Journal of Business Research, 125*, 772–779.

Shaikh, N. (2023). Generative AI use cases for e-commerce. *International Journal of Computer Science and Mobile Computing, 12*, 10–14.

Shrestha, Y. R., Ben-Menahem, S. M., & Von Krogh, G. (2019). Organizational decision-making structures in the age of artificial intelligence. *California Management Review, 61*(4), 66–83.

Simkute, A., Tankelevitch, L., Kewenig, V., Scott, A. E., Sellen, A., & Rintel, S. (2024). Ironies of Generative AI: Understanding and mitigating productivity loss in human-AI interaction. *International Journal of Human–Computer Interaction*, 1–22.

Simon, H. A. (1987). Making management decisions: The role of intuition and emotion. *Academy of Management Perspectives, 1*(1), 57–64.

Solaiman, B., & Cohen, I. G. (2024). A framework for health, AI and the law. In *Research handbook on health, AI and the law* (pp. 1–19). Edward Elgar.

Sturm, T., Gerlach, J. P., Pumplun, L., Mesbah, N., Peters, F., Tauchert, C., ... & Buxmann, P. (2021). Coordinating human and machine learning for effective organizational learning. *MIS Quarterly, 45*(3), 1581–1602.

Taherizadeh, S., Jones, A. C., Taylor, I., Zhao, Z., & Stankovski, V. (2018). Monitoring self-adaptive applications within edge computing frameworks: A state-of-the-art review. *Journal of Systems and Software, 136*, 19–38.

Tambe, P., Cappelli, P., & Yakubovich, V. (2019). Artificial intelligence in human resources management: Challenges and a path forward. *California Management Review, 61*(4), 15–42.

Teece, D. J. (2018). Profiting from innovation in the digital economy: Enabling technologies, standards, and licensing models in the wireless world. *Research Policy, 47*(8), 1367–1387.

Tighe, S. A., Ball, K., Kensing, F., Kayser, L., Rawstorn, J. C., & Maddison, R. (2020). Toward a digital platform for the self-management of noncommunicable disease: Systematic review of platform-like interventions. *Journal of Medical Internet Research, 22*(10), e16774.

Ting, D. S. W., Carin, L., Dzau, V., & Wong, T. Y. (2020). Digital technology and COVID-19. *Nature Medicine, 26*(4), 459–461.

Tsagkaris, C., Hoian, A. V., Ahmad, S., Essar, M. Y., Campbell, L. W., Grobusch, L., Angelopoulos, T., & Kalaitzidis, K. (2021). Using telemedicine for a lower carbon footprint in healthcare: A twofold tale of healing. *The Journal of Climate Change and Health, 1*, 100006.

Tseng, M. L., Chang, C. H., Lin, C. W. R., Wu, K. J., Chen, Q., Xia, L., & Xue, B. (2020). Future trends and guidance for the triple bottom line and sustainability: A data driven bibliometric analysis. *Environmental Science and Pollution Research, 27*, 33543–33567.

Uzunidis, D. (2009). Innovation, growth and sustainable development: General presentation. *Journal of Innovation Economics, 1*, 5–11.

Van den Heuvel, R., Kapadia, A., Stirling, C., & Zhou, J. (2018). *Medical devices 2030*. KPMG.

Van Laar, E., Van Deursen, A. J., Van Dijk, J. A., & De Haan, J. (2020). Determinants of 21st-century skills and 21st-century digital skills for workers: A systematic literature review. *Sage Open, 10*(1), 2158244019900176.

Verhoef, P. C., Broekhuizen, T., Bart, Y., Bhattacharya, A., Dong, J. Q., Fabian, N., & Haenlein, M. (2021). Digital transformation: A multidisciplinary reflection and research agenda. *Journal of Business Research, 122*, 889–901.

Vial, G. (2019). Understanding digital transformation: A review and a research agenda. *The Journal of Strategic Information Systems, 28*(2), 118–144.

Vyas, D., Chisalita, C. M., & Dix, A. (2017). Organizational affordances: A structuration theory approach to affordances. *Interacting with Computers, 29*(2), 117–131.

Wang, Q., Su, M., Zhang, M., & Li, R. (2021). Integrating digital technologies and public health to fight Covid-19 pandemic: Key technologies, applications, challenges and outlook of digital healthcare. *International Journal of Environmental Research and Public Health, 18*(11), 6053.

Warner, K. S., & Wäger, M. (2019). Building dynamic capabilities for digital transformation: An ongoing process of strategic renewal. *Long Range Planning, 52*(3), 326–349.

Woods, S. A., Ahmed, S., Nikolaou, I., Costa, A. C., & Anderson, N. R. (2020). Personnel selection in the digital age: A review of validity and applicant reactions, and future research challenges. *European Journal of Work and Organizational Psychology, 29*(1), 64–77.

World Commission on Environment and Development (WCED). (1987). *Brundtland report (Britannica)*. World Commission on Environment and Development. https://www.britannica.com/topic/Brundtland-Report

Yang, Y., Siau, K., Xie, W., & Sun, Y. (2022). Smart health: Intelligent healthcare systems in the metaverse, artificial intelligence, and data science era. *Journal of Organizational and End User Computing (JOEUC), 34*(1), 1–14.

Yang, Y., Zheng, X., Guo, W., Liu, X., & Chang, V. (2019). Privacy-preserving smart IoT-based healthcare big data storage and self-adaptive access control system. *Information Sciences, 479*, 567–592.

Yeng, P. K., Nweke, L. O., Woldaregay, A. Z., Yang, B., & Snekkenes, E. A. (2021). Data-driven and artificial intelligence (AI) approach for modelling and analyzing healthcare security practice: A systematic review. In *Intelligent systems and applications: Proceedings of the 2020 intelligent systems conference (IntelliSys) volume 1* (pp. 1–18). Springer.

Yim, D., Khuntia, J., Parameswaran, V., & Meyers, A. (2024). Preliminary evidence of the use of Generative AI in health care clinical services: Systematic narrative review. *JMIR Medical Informatics, 12*(1), e52073.

Yin, Y., & Qin, S. F. (2019). A smart performance measurement approach for collaborative design in Industry 4.0. *Advances in Mechanical Engineering, 11*(1), 1687814018822570.

Yu, K. H., Beam, A. L., & Kohane, I. S. (2018). Artificial intelligence in healthcare. *Nature Biomedical Engineering, 2*(10), 719–731.

Yumnam, V. (2024). Manipur's journey towards the health SDGS: What's achieved and what more is needed? *Indian Journal of Community Medicine, 49*(1), 18–21.

Zaltman, G., & Wallendorf, M. (1979). *Consumer behavior: Basic findings and management implications*. Wiley.

Zhang, P., & Kamel Boulos, M. N. (2023). Generative AI in medicine and healthcare: Promises, opportunities and challenges. *Future Internet, 15*(9), 286.

Ziyadin, S., Ermekbaeva, B., Supugaliyeva, G., & Doszhan, R. (2018). Transformation of basic indicators of socio-economic processes in the digital economy. In *Proceedings of the 31st IBIMA 2018* (pp. 2009–2017 (2)).

Zollo, M., Bettinazzi, E. L., Neumann, K., & Snoeren, P. (2016). Toward a comprehensive model of organizational evolution: Dynamic capabilities for innovation and adaptation of the enterprise model. *Global Strategy Journal, 6*(3), 225–244.

Chapter 3
Inter-organisational Network in the Healthcare Sector: Insights from Precision Medicine in Oncology

Abstract In this chapter, the authors provide an overview of the definition, evolution, and the impact of inter-organisational networks in healthcare, known as *care networks*. In doing this, the author reviewed the main literature about the topic, selecting as relevant the conceptual frameworks developed by Menear et al. (*Health Research Policy and Systems, 17*, 1–13, 2019) and Denicolai and Previtali (*Technological Forecasting and Social Change, 151*, 119767, 2020). In Sect. 3.2, the focus shifts to precision medicine (PM), the research setting of this book, exploring the current state of care networks in Italy. Due to the exploratory nature of the topic, the author has mapped the state of the art of such networks in Italy by conducting semi-structured interviews with industry experts during a 6-month stage at Kelyon (https://kelyon.com), heavily involved in defining PM networks. These interviews acted as the foundation for developing the theoretical background of the book.

Keywords Healthcare · Care network · Precision medicine · Value co-creation · Italy

3.1 The Spread of the Care Network in Healthcare

3.1.1 Definition and Evolution in Italy

Healthcare is one of the main sectors influenced by the spread of the inter-organisational model (Gray, 1985; Van Bueren et al., 2003), aiming to coordinate care for heterogeneous patients (Palumbo et al., 2015). Moreover, it is characterised by a high level of complexity, emphasising the need for collaborative planning among stakeholders to plan care, referrals, and shared patients' information (Sheaff & Schofield, 2016). On the other hand, healthcare systems face pressure to allocate resources effectively and demonstrate service quality to all stakeholders. Thus, national healthcare systems—especially in oncology—are adopting regional

A. Bastone, *The Power of Generative Artificial Intelligence for Value Co-Creation in Healthcare*, SpringerBriefs in Health Care Management and Economics, https://doi.org/10.1007/978-3-032-14298-6_3

oncology networks characterised by higher flexibility and adaptability. These models are innovative tools to address care needs through: (1) clinical outcomes optimisation, (2) evidence-based healthcare system development, (3) cost containment, (4) knowledge sharing, (5) equitable access to care, and (6) resources optimisation (Ferlie et al., 2010; Howard et al., 2008). Particularly, they ensure a multidisciplinary approach through diagnostic-therapeutic-assistance paths shared by the network nodes (PDTA), ensuring continuity of care, timely interventions, and reduced waiting lists.

Focusing on Italy, several regions have adopted a network approach to optimise resource allocation (Secundo et al., 2021) and enhance care quality (Russo-Spena et al., 2019). For instance, Tuscany institutionalised the *"coordination and integration of interventions within the regional framework"* in 1998 (Fioretto et al., 2016). However, Piedmont was the first one to concretely implement an oncology network in 2000, extending it to Valle d'Aosta in 2003. In this context, the Campania region established the Campania Oncology Network (ROC) in 2016 to define well-structured diagnostic-therapeutic pathways, thereby reducing diagnostic and therapeutic delays and ensuring equity of access, appropriateness of care settings, and integration between hospitals and the territory (Crispo et al., 2022). While empirical evidence demonstrates the benefits of these models, their adoption remains uneven across the country, underscoring the need for synergy and effective national coordination.

3.1.2 Co-creating Value in Healthcare Network

As discussed in Chap. 1, in inter-organisational networks, the concept of value is crucial. In healthcare, the need for coordination (Palumbo et al., 2020) implies that value is co-created through collaboration among all the actors involved (Vargo & Lusch, 2014), making interaction and information sharing crucial for generating value for both patients and healthcare systems. Thus, patients take on an active role in their care path, improving their empowerment and centrality (Buccoliero, 2010). In this context, the healthcare system is viewed as a set of interconnected actors, marking a shift from a network perspective to an ecosystem perspective (Denicolai & Previtali, 2020), where digital technologies play a key role in enabling faster communication between participants (Masucci et al., 2021).

As Friedman et al. (2015) attested, the need to delineate a value-driven and digitally oriented health system paves the way to the development of so-called Learning Health Systems (LHS), defined as *"a vision for an integrated health system in which progress in science, informatics, and care culture align to generate new knowledge as an ongoing, natural by-product of the care experience, and seamlessly refine and deliver best practices for continuous improvement in health and healthcare"* (IOM, 2011; Smith et al., 2012).

The Agency for Healthcare Research and Quality complements this definition as *"a health system in which internal data and experience are systematically integrated with external evidence and knowledge is put into practice. As a result, patients get higher quality, safer, more efficient care, and healthcare delivery organisations become better places to work"*. These systems, therefore, emphasise learning processes that, when embedded in daily healthcare practices, drive continuous enhancement in care and health by maximising value creation (Polese et al., 2021). They foster continuous improvement through an iterative cycle that integrates data, knowledge, and practices (Nelson & Reeves, 2023).

Drawing on some empirical evidence, Menear et al. (2019) proposed a conceptual framework for value co-creation within LHSs (Fig. 3.1). Notably, authors started from the assumption that LHSs are dynamic ecosystems in which scientific, social, technological, political, legal, and ethical dimensions—considered the pillars of LHSs—are aligned to embed learning and improvement processes into daily practices and routines of healthcare organisations. In this view, the value results from balancing *"impacts on patient and provider experience, population health and health system costs"* (Zomahoun et al., 2024). Additionally, these systems can operate on a regional, national, or international scale across three levels: (1) *micro level*—encompassing organisations that produce and deliver healthcare services; (2) *meso level*—where shared objectives are stated; (3) *macro level*—focused on planning at the population scale (Menear et al., 2019).

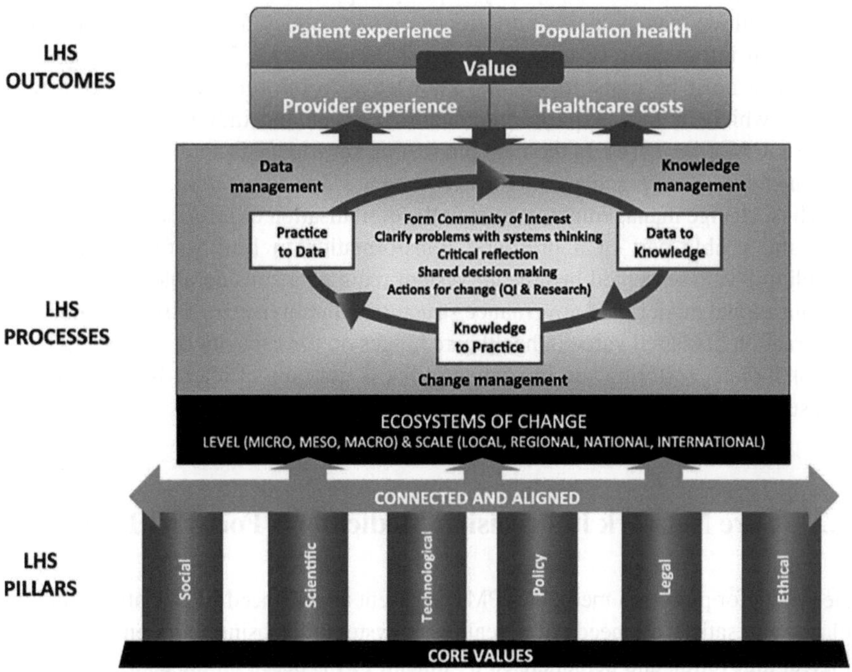

Fig. 3.1 Conceptual framework for value-creating learning health systems. Source(s): Menear, M., Blanchette, M. A., Demers-Payette, O., & Roy, D. (2019). A framework for value-creating learning health systems. *Health Research Policy and Systems, 17*, 1–13

Zomahoun et al. (2024) identified core values underpinning LHS, including accessibility, adaptability, cooperative and participative leadership, governance, inclusiveness, person-centredness, privacy, scientific integrity, transparency, and value in healthcare. This underscores the need for healthcare ecosystems to involve all stakeholders—focusing on patients' needs and expectations (Brooks et al., 2017)—and to promote value co-creation and patient empowerment (Buccoliero, 2010). Equally relevant is defining shared responsibility to ensure a fair and transparent healthcare service, positioning value as the "driving force" of health systems (Lavis et al., 2018; Menear et al., 2019).

As previously mentioned, LHS is supported by six main pillars. Among these, technology is central as its capacity to stimulate learning, allowing for the gathering, aggregation, analysis, and action on high-quality clinical data. On the other hand, continuous training of the healthcare professionals is key to improving the quality of care, as well as the collaboration among the ecosystem's actors—including policymakers—who must establish laws and regulations that enable learning while safeguarding privacy and ethics (Nelson & Reeves, 2023).

Furthermore, the framework highlights that learning processes can follow three basic phases (Friedman et al., 2015): (1) *practice to data* (P2D), (2) *data to knowledge* (D2K), and (3) *knowledge to practice* (K2P). In this view, fostering learning relies on the appropriate management of huge data generated, supported by monitoring systems to ensure data quality. Equally important is technology implementation that allows stakeholders at different levels to collect, transfer, synthesise, and store such information (Daniel et al., 2017; Mandl et al., 2014). Once gathered, these data must be transformed into knowledge to inform decision-making processes, which in turn requires interaction between the individual stakeholders (Forest & Martin, 2018). In the final phase, this knowledge is applied to drive innovation and improve practices, thereby enhancing value co-creation.

Thus, change management is crucial; the digitalisation of information represents only the visible part of a profound transformation in healthcare management. Building a value-oriented healthcare system requires a considerable change in the organisational models and governance structures (Tamblyn et al., 2016). Ultimately, the creation of shared value in healthcare hinges on the capacity of all stakeholders to collaborate, fostering service delivery that is not only efficient but also ethical and sustainable (Van den Broek et al., 2018).

3.2 Care Network in Precision Medicine: A Focus on Italy

Networks for precision medicine (PM) represent an advanced organisational model planned to satisfy the needs of a healthcare system increasingly driven by technological innovation and personalised treatment. PM is based on the analysis of individual genetic, environmental, and lifestyle variances, aiming to reveal the molecular mechanisms of diseases and to optimise therapeutic strategies (Faulkner et al., 2020). Notably, this approach is valuable in complex fields such as oncology, immunology, rare diseases, cardiovascular and respiratory illnesses, neurological disorders, and infectious diseases (Mateo et al., 2022). Despite its potential, adopting PM faces meaningful barriers, including the high costs of diagnostic and therapeutic technologies, difficulties in performing clinical trials with small patient groups, and regulatory doubts. The Hub & Spoke network model represents a potential solution to address these issues and promote fairness and equity (Stenzinger et al., 2023). Particularly, this model is characterised by a clear division of roles. Hubs represent highly specialised centres of excellence furnished with advanced technologies and multidisciplinary teams. The Spokes are peripheral centres responsible for guaranteeing territorial proximity, providing essential and medium-complexity services, sending biological samples to the Hubs, and implementing the treatments (Fasola et al., 2022). Networks structured according to this model ensure several benefits, including economies of scale and scope, which reduce costs (Elrod & Fortenberry, 2017). Additionally, they enhance the system's overall effectiveness, ensuring easy access to healthcare services (Hoeyer, 2019).

The peculiarities of PM qualify it as a dynamic and interconnected innovation ecosystem, characterised by a multi-actor and multi-directional nature. Thus, PM can be considered as a learning health system oriented towards the prevention and control of health, focused on continuous learning and new knowledge generation (Denicolai & Previtali, 2020; Garcia-Quevedo et al., 2011; Menear et al., 2019; Shaikh et al., 2014). Based on these premises, the empirical analysis of Denicolai and Previtali (2020) highlights that PM significantly impacts the health sector value chain, less based on linear processes and cascading sequences of activities (Kim et al., 2010), paving the way for continuous cycles and dynamic linkages within adaptive ecosystems (Fig. 3.2).

Particularly, their model attests that prevention and prediction models are relevant where research, diagnosis, and treatment overlap, with porous boundaries between their functions. It is key to continuously monitor each stage, even outside healthcare facilities, by integrating data from all the stakeholders (e.g. patients, pharmaceutical companies, and research institutes). This activates a virtuous and continuous cycle of improvement in the prevention and prediction processes. However, this model also faces criticism due to institutional, organisational, and ethical barriers that can hinder the introduction of innovations in highly regulated sectors, such as healthcare.

In Italy, some major PM networks have developed. AZ Fastnet is a PM network supported by pharmaceutical companies, developed in Southern Italy in 2009 as EGFR Fastnet to support molecular testing for lung cancer, with great attention to the EGFR gene mutation. In a second phase, the network expanded to include ovarian cancer tests and liquid biopsies. On the other hand, Keras Active, supported by Merck Serono and dedicated to metastatic colorectal cancer, operated from 2008 to 2012 and played a key role in introducing molecular testing of KRAS and NRAS genes into clinical practice. Although it no longer operates, its relevance remains central to developing diagnosis networks in Italy.

Among the networks emerging from international clinical projects is the Europe-wide Precision Medicine network, EPROPA, sponsored by the patient association

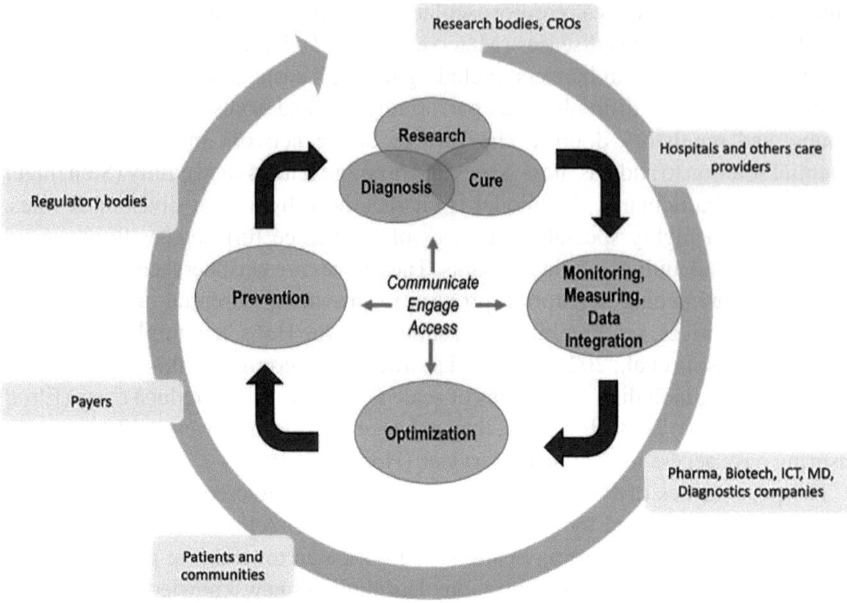

Fig. 3.2 Healthcare value chain as a continuous learning and optimisation loop. Source(s): Denicolai, S., & Previtali, P. (2020). Precision Medicine: Implications for value chains and business models in life sciences. *Technological Forecasting and Social Change, 151*, 119767

Walce Onlus. It provides European centres free access to next-generation genetic sequencing (NGS) tests for lung cancer and offers logistical and economic support for patients and caregivers. It's an innovative approach to bridging the gap between patients and hospitals that can provide specific treatments. "ROME" is an interregional study based on the establishment of a collaborative Molecular Tumour Board. It brings together experts from various Italian institutions who meet weekly to discuss clinical cases referred to Foundation Medicine, a company specialising in molecular DNA characterisation. Data are then fed back to hospitals to optimise therapeutic decisions. This model illustrates the sharing of expertise to ensure a national approach to high-quality diagnostics and treatment.

The ATLAS project is a collaborative database inspired by platforms such as MyCancerGenome in the United States, which is built on molecular knowledge. It covers a database of Italian centres focusing on genetic mutations and their interactions with other biological markers (e.g. PD-L1) primarily in lung cancer. This project contributes to research enhancing the effectiveness of personalised care in clinical practice. Finally, the Luce Network is a European collaborative network that helps patients in identifying and accessing active clinical trials at several institutions.

Despite the major advances that have been achieved, several challenges remain. Notably, the high cost restricts PM networks' adoption, while the lack of unique regulatory standards results in fragmented implementation across regions.

Furthermore, insufficient ad hoc funding inhibits these networks from reaching their full potential. There is also a burning need for continuous training of healthcare professionals to keep pace with the rapid evolution of technologies.

References

Brooks, D., Douglas, M., Aggarwal, N., Prabhakaran, S., Holden, K., & Mack, D. (2017). Developing a framework for integrating health equity into the learning health system. *Learning Health Systems, 1*(3), e10029.

Buccoliero, L. (2010). E-health 2.0. Tecnologie per il patient empowerment. *Mondo Digitale, 4*, 3–17.

Crispo, A., Rivieccio, G., Cataldo, L., Coluccia, S., Luongo, A., Coppola, E., Grimaldi, M., Montagnese, C., Nocerino, F., D'Errico, D., Celentano, E., Saviano, R., Bastone, A., Baglio, G., De Angelis, C., Ciardiello, F., Avallone, A., Cassata, A., Costanzo, R., … Pignata, S. (2022). New approach to implement cancer patient care: The valutazione percorso rete oncologica campana (ValPeROC)-experience from an Italian oncology network. *European Journal of Cancer Care, 31*(6), e13736.

Daniel, C., Ouagne, D., Sadou, E., Paris, N., Hussain, S., Jaulent, M. C., & Kalra, D. (2017). Cross border semantic interoperability for learning health systems: The EHR4CR semantic resources and services. *Learning Health System, 1*(1), e10014.

Denicolai, S., & Previtali, P. (2020). Precision medicine: Implications for value chains and business models in life sciences. *Technological Forecasting and Social Change, 151*, 119767.

Elrod, J. K., & Fortenberry, J. L. (2017). The hub-and-spoke organization design: An avenue for serving patients well. *BMC Health Services Research, 17*, 25–33.

Fasola, G., Pelizzari, G., Barducci, M. C., Garattini, S. K., Poletto, E., Cesselli, D., De Maglio, G., Bonura, S., Cozzi, M., Fabbro, D., Virdis, L., Toffoletti, E., Curcio, F., Regattin, L., & Tozzi, V. D. (2022). Molecular Tumor Board: A bottom-up approach as method for change. *Journal of Clinical Oncology, 40*(16_suppl).

Faulkner, E., Holtorf, A. P., Liu, C. Y., Lin, H., Biltaj, E., Brixner, D., Walton, S., Barr, C., Oberg, J., Shandhu, G., Siebert, U., Snyder, S. R., Tiwana, S., Watkins, J., IJzerman, M. J., & Payne, K. (2020). Being precise about precision medicine: What should value frameworks incorporate to address precision medicine? A report of the personalized precision medicine special interest group. *Value in Health, 23*(5), 529–539.

Ferlie, E., Fitzgerald, L., McGivern, G., Dopson, S., & Exworthy, M. (2010). *Networks in health care: A comparative study of their management, impact and performance*. Report for the National Institute for Health Research Service Delivery and Organisation Programme.

Fioretto, L., Cheli, S., & Amunni, G. (2016). La riforma ei Dipartimenti oncologici. *Salute e Territorio, 209*, 878–883.

Forest, P. G., & Martin, D. (2018). *Fit for purpose: Findings and recommendations of the external review of the Pan-Canadian health organizations: Summary report*. Health Canada.

Friedman, C., Rubin, J., Brown, J., Buntin, M., Corn, M., Etheredge, L., Gunter, C., Musen, M., Platt, R., Stead, W., Sullivan, K., & Van Houweling, D. (2015). Toward a science of learning systems: A research agenda for the high-functioning Learning Health System. *Journal of the American Medical Informatics Association, 22*(1), 43–50.

Garcia-Quevedo, J., Mas-Verdu, F., & Soriano, D. R. (2011). The heterogeneity of services and the differential effects on business and territorial innovation. *International Journal of Technology Management, 54*(1), 80–93.

Gray, B. (1985). Conditions facilitating interorganizational collaboration. *Human Relations, 38*(10), 911–936.

Hoeyer, K. (2019). Data as promise: Reconfiguring Danish public health through personalized medicine. *Social Studies of Science, 49*(4), 531–555.

Howard, M., Goertzen, J., Kaczorowski, J., Hutchison, B., Morris, K., Thabane, L., Levine, M., & Papaioannou, A. (2008). Emergency department and walk-in clinic use in models of primary care practice with different after-hours accessibility in Ontario. *Healthcare Policy, 4*(1), 73.

Institute of Medicine (IOM). (2011). Digital infrastructure for the learning health system: The foundation for continuous improvement in health and health care. In C. Grossman, B. Powers, & J. M. McGinnis (Eds.), *The foundation for continuous improvement in health and health care. Workshop series summary* (pp. 1–311). National Academies Press.

Kim, J. Y., Rhatigan, J., Jain, S. H., Weintraub, R., & Porter, M. E. (2010). From a declaration of values to the creation of value in global health: A report from Harvard University's Global Health Delivery Project. *Global Public Health, 5*(2), 181–188.

Lavis, J. N., Gauvin, F. P., Mattison, C. A., Moat, K. A., Waddell, K., Wilson, M. G., & Reid, R. (2018, December). *Rapid synbook—Creating rapid-learning health systems in Canada.* McMaster Health Forum.

Mandl, K. D., Kohane, I. S., McFadden, D., Weber, G. M., Natter, M., Mandel, J., Schneeweiss, S., Weiler, S., Klann, J. G., Bickel, J., Adams, W. G., Ge, Y., Zhou, X., Perkins, J., Marsolo, K., Bernstam, E., Showalter, J., Quarshie, A., Ofili E., … Murphy, S. N. (2014). Scalable collaborative infrastructure for a learning healthcare system (SCILHS): Architecture. *Journal of the American Medical Informatics Association, 21*(4), 615–620.

Masucci, A., Megaro, A., & Sirianni, C. A. (2021). The role of new technologies in value co-creation processes: Healthcare management and the national health system as a system of services. *Journal of Service Science and Management, 14*(2), 189–212.

Mateo, J., Steuten, L., Aftimos, P., André, F., Davies, M., Garralda, E., Geissler, J., Husereau, D., Martinez-Lopez, I., Normanno, N., Reis-Filho, J. S., Stefani, S., Thomas, D. M., Westphalen, C. B., & Voest, E. (2022). Delivering precision oncology to patients with cancer. *Nature Medicine, 28*(4), 658–665.

Menear, M., Blanchette, M. A., Demers-Payette, O., & Roy, D. (2019). A framework for value-creating learning health systems. *Health Research Policy and Systems, 17*, 1–13.

Nelson, W., & Reeves, S. (2023). A learning healthcare systems approach. *Healthcare Executive, 38*(5), 30–31.

Palumbo, C., Volpe, U., Matanov, A., Priebe, S., & Giacco, D. (2015). Social networks of patients with psychosis: A systematic review. *BMC Research Notes, 8*, 1–12.

Palumbo, R., Manesh, M. F., Pellegrini, M. M., & Flamini, G. (2020). Exploiting inter-organizational relationships in health care: A bibliometric analysis and literature review. *Administrative Sciences, 10*(3), 57.

Polese, F., Troisi, O., Grimaldi, M., & Loia, F. (2021). Reinterpreting governance in smart cities: An ecosystem-based view. In A. Visvizi & R. P. del Hoyo (Eds.), *Smart cities and the UN SDGs* (pp. 71–89). Elsevier.

Russo-Spena, T., Mele, C., & Marzullo, M. (2019). Practising value innovation through artificial intelligence: The IBM Watson case. *Journal of Creating Value, 5*(1), 11–24.

Secundo, G., Shams, S. R., & Nucci, F. (2021). Digital technologies and collective intelligence for healthcare ecosystem: Optimising Internet of Things adoption for pandemic management. *Journal of Business Research, 131*, 563–572.

Shaikh, A. R., Butte, A. J., Schully, S. D., Dalton, W. S., Khoury, M. J., & Hesse, B. W. (2014). Collaborative biomedicine in the age of big data: The case of cancer. *Journal of Medical Internet Research, 16*(4), e101.

Sheaff, R., & Schofield, J. (2016). Inter-organizational networks in health care. In E. Ferlie, K. Montgomery, & A. R. Pedersen (Eds.), *The Oxford handbook of health care management* (pp. 434–458). Oxford Academic.

Smith, M., Saunders, R., Stuckhardt, L., & McGinnis, J. (Eds.). (2012). *Best care at lower cost: The path to continuously learning health care in America* (1st ed., pp. 1–450). National Academies Press. http://www.iom.edu/bestcare

Stenzinger, A., Moltzen, E. K., Winkler, E., Molnar-Gabor, F., Malek, N., Costescu, A., Jensen, B. N., Nowak, F., Pinto, C., Ottersen, O. P., Schirmacher, P., Nordborg, J., Seufferlein, T., Fröhling, S., Edsjö, A., Garcia-Foncillas, J., Normanno, N., Lundgren, B., Friedman, M., … Rosenquist, R. (2023). Implementation of precision medicine in healthcare—A European perspective. *Journal of Internal Medicine, 294*(4), 437–454.

Tamblyn, R., McMahon, M., Nadigel, J., & Dunning, B. (2016). Health system transformation through research innovation. *HealthcarePapers, 16*(Special Issue).

Van Bueren, E. M., Klijn, E. H., & Koppenjan, J. F. (2003). Dealing with wicked problems in networks: Analyzing an environmental debate from a network perspective. *Journal of Public Administration Research and Theory, 13*(2), 193–212.

Van den Broek, J., Boselie, P., & Paauwe, J. (2018). Cooperative innovation through a talent management pool: A qualitative study on coopetition in healthcare. *European Management Journal, 36*(1), 135–144.

Vargo, S. L., & Lusch, R. F. (2014). Inversions of service-dominant logic. *Marketing Theory, 14*(3), 239–248.

Zomahoun, H. T. V., Giroux, C. M., Boies, S., Bush, P., Alkhaldi, M., Talla, P. K., Poitras, M.- E., Couturier, Y., & Ahmed, S. (2024). Evaluating health organization readiness for implementing a learning health system: Literature review to inform questionnaire development.

Chapter 4
Investigating the Role of Generative Artificial Intelligence in Value Creation

Abstract This chapter describes the methodological approach adopted. Particularly, the research methodology is presented, with particular emphasis on the consistency between the research objectives and methods. Section 4.3 provides an overview of data collection and analysis methods, with specific attention to the selection of key informants, the interview protocol, and sources of evidence.

Section 4.5 describes the thematic analysis' main findings. The data analysis allowed for the development of a conceptual framework to map the key stages of the value co-creation in healthcare networks. Notably, it emphasises the role of GenAI and uncovers the main barriers and facilitators to its implementation.

Keywords Exploratory analysis · Thematic analysis · Conceptual framework · Research agenda

4.1 Introduction

This chapter aims to illustrate the exploratory analysis conducted by highlighting the methodological steps followed. The author investigated the potential role of GenAI as a facilitator or barrier in value co-creation processes within PM networks through a multi-level perspective encompassing the micro, meso, and macro levels of analysis. Additionally, the author conducted a bibliometric analysis to identify patterns and new themes in the literature on GenAI.

The study followed three main phases: (1) data collection, exploring the key informants *"how—and sometimes why—construct meanings and action in specific situations"* (Charmaz, 2008), (2) data analysis, and (3) conceptual framework development. The author identified multiple sources of evidence to guarantee triangulation, including: (1) key informant interviews, (2) official online documentation, (3) public declarations, and (4) archival records (Yin, 2009). Thus, a thematic analysis was conducted due to its potential to address exploratory intentions.

A. Bastone, *The Power of Generative Artificial Intelligence for Value Co-Creation in Healthcare*, SpringerBriefs in Health Care Management and Economics, https://doi.org/10.1007/978-3-032-14298-6_4

Finally, the study put forth a new conceptual framework based on the empirical investigation. Mostly, its originality is derived from its extension and integration of the conceptual frameworks proposed by Menear et al. (2019) and Denicolai and Previtali (2020). The first describes the process of value co-creation in healthcare networks; the second clarifies the role of PM in value chain transformation.

4.2 Research Setting

One of the primary objectives of clinical trials and medical practice is to enhance the quality of care and ensure adherence by concentrating on the distinctive characteristics of each patient. Since the 1990s, the concept of evidence-based medicine has gained traction. However, identifying the most appropriate treatment for a specific condition while considering the variety of patient characteristics is one of the most significant issues for healthcare experts.

In this context, precision medicine (PM) is a recent field of study that aims to enhance clinical decision-making processes by leveraging the variability inherent in biological characteristics. This paradigm is based on the development of personalised treatments according to individual characteristics, with the integration of genetic, molecular, environmental, and clinical information. The Food and Drug Administration characterises it as *"an innovative approach to tailoring disease prevention and treatment that takes into account differences in people's genes, environments, and lifestyles"*.

Consequently, PM can be categorised as a form of personalised medicine that is having a transformative effect on several fields, including oncology. In this field, this approach allows for the identification of tumour characteristics, such as genetic mutations or molecular alterations. This, in turn, facilitates the identification of the most appropriate therapy for each patient.

Nevertheless, the high expense of precision treatments poses a considerable obstacle to the healthcare system, necessitating the establishment of a well-organised structure that encourages cooperation amongst the different system stakeholders (e.g. laboratories, software houses, pharmaceutical companies, regional institutions, and biotechnology companies). Consequently, the paradigm of inter-organisational networks emerges as a suitable model for large-scale PM implementation, given its ability to reduce the time lag between scientific discovery and application. Networks facilitate interdisciplinary professional collaboration, thereby enabling the real-time sharing of data, resources, and knowledge through digital infrastructures. For PM networks, the capacity to engender value at the therapeutic, financial, and social levels is among its most crucial features. From a clinical perspective, these agents have been shown to mitigate the risk of adverse effects while facilitating more focused and efficient treatments, thereby enhancing patient health outcomes. From a financial perspective, they can assist in minimising waste and optimising the distribution of healthcare resources. Finally, they serve to reduce healthcare disparities on a societal level by ensuring a greater number of patients have access to cutting-edge treatments. Consequently, for patients and other healthcare stakeholders, the concept of value co-creation is of paramount importance.

4.3 Research Method

When we have an exploratory intention, a key informant interview is the most suitable technique because it is useful for exploring emerging themes and obtaining a deeper understanding of a system or process (Cohen et al., 2002). Particularly, it aims to involve electing informants who qualify as "experts" on a specific topic (Lokot, 2021; Taylor & Blake, 2015).

In this book the author conducted 15 online interviews with key informants lasting 60 min each to better comprehend the role of GenAI in the value co-creation process within PM networks. Thus, interviews were recorded, transcribed, and translated into English, trying to guarantee the original meaning of the quotes. A purposeful sample approach was followed (Suri, 2011). Additionally, the snowball sampling technique was shadowed, asking the original target of the informant to pinpoint potential new participants who met the eligibility criteria (Bogner et al., 2009, p. 2; Naderifar et al., 2017; Pahwa et al., 2023; Parker et al., 2019).

Table 4.1 offers an overview of the sample. Since PM networks are nodes of a multi-actor and dynamic ecosystem, interviews were conducted with physicians, managers of pharmaceutical companies and software houses to get a holistic view.

Particularly, adopting an ecosystem approach, the author developed the interview protocol considering three levels of analysis (Table 4.2): (1) *micro level*—to investigate the individual node (e.g. laboratories, providers, and pharmaceutical companies); (2) *meso level*—to explore the collaboration between nodes; (3) *macro level*—to analyse the influence of GenAI on the whole ecosystem and public health. Lastly, the potential benefits and risks associated with the use of GenAI were explored.

As recommended by Yin (2009), secondary sources of evidence were used to construct validity from official online documentation, public statements, and archival records. Table 4.3 shows the main constructs and sources of information used. The collected data were analysed using thematic analysis by implementing NVivo software (Braun & Clarke, 2006; Cohen et al., 2002; Joffe, 2011). The thematic analysis aims to highlight the most salient configurations of meaning in the collected datasets, including affective, cognitive, and symbolic dimensions (Joffe,

Table 4.1 Sample of key informants

Position	Numbers
Head of the Pathological Anatomy Lab	10
Software house manager	3
Pharma companies' manager	2

Source(s): Author research

Table 4.2 Interview protocol

Level of analysis	Question
Micro level	Could the introduction of GenAI tools be a game-changer for your work? If so, how?
	Could GenAI have an impact on diagnosis? If so, how?
	Could GenAI help personalise treatments? If so, how?
	Could GenAI influence the R&D process? If so, how?
	Could GenAI affect patient engagement? If so, how?
Meso level	Could GenAI affect collaboration between nodes of the network? If so, how?
	Could GenAI affect communications between nodes of the network? If so, how?
	Could GenAI affect the readability of shared data? If so, how?
Macro level	Could GenAI influence how healthcare networks co-create value?
	In terms of quality of care, what impact can GenAI have on public health?
	In terms of costs, what impact can GenAI have on public health?
Pros and cons	What are the benefits of using GenAI in PM networks?
	How to maximise the benefits of GenAI in PM networks?
	What are the risks and challenges of using GenAI in PM networks?
	How to mitigate risks of using GenAI in PM networks?

Source(s): Author research

Table 4.3 Main constructs and sources of evidence

Constructs	– Adoption of inter-organisational network model in PM – Technological change management as a pillar of value co-creation in the PM network
Expert Interviews	Questions about potential impact of GenAI on the PM network along three levels (micro, meso, and macro)
Official online documentation	– International Network Medicine Consortium documentations – European Commission documentations
Archival records	Documentations of pharmaceutical companies and software house official websites
Public declarations	– AIFA declarations – Heal Italia members declarations

Source(s): Author's research

2011). Particularly, an inductive approach was adopted following Braun and Clarke's (2006) six main steps. Finally, the identified themes were interpreted to develop a conceptual framework following a grounded approach (Charmaz, 2015).

4.4 Bibliometric Analysis

A pivotal technique for quantitatively evaluating research production is bibliometric analysis. As posited by Aria and Cuccurullo (2017), this approach entails *"the utilisation of mathematical and statistical methodologies in the context of books and alternative modes of communication"*, thereby facilitating researchers in discerning patterns, gaps, and opportunities within the extant literature. De Oliveira et al. (2019) posit that bibliometric analysis is a particularly efficacious tool for identifying uncharted territory and directing researchers towards potential lines of inquiry. To enhance their ideas and build upon a robust foundation of current knowledge, researchers must analyse the state of the art (Gläser & Laudel, 2015). The application of bibliometric methods has been demonstrated to facilitate the formulation of research questions, the establishment of future objectives, and the advancement of a given field (Campbell et al., 2010; Gläser & Laudel, 2015). To identify patterns and new themes in the literature on GenAI in the service sector, a bibliometric analysis is, therefore, appropriate as the initial stage of this research. The author adhered to the De Oliveira et al. (2019) protocol (see Fig. 4.1). Scopus, a comprehensive academic database, was utilised for this investigation. Due to its extensive collection of scholarly sources, comprehensive coverage of scientific publications, and robust bibliometric indicators, Scopus was selected (Pranckutė, 2021). To ensure a comprehensive overview of the extant literature, the search was not restricted by time or date. The search string was carefully constructed to focus on key themes: TITLE-ABS-KEY ("Generative Artificial Intelligence" OR "Artificial Intelligence" AND "healthcare network" OR "service industry" AND "value" OR "value creation" OR "value co-creation"). This approach yielded a total of 132 relevant articles.

The author then proceeded to conduct the bibliometric analysis in accordance with the methodology established by Aria and Cuccurullo (2017). It was hypothesised that statistics such as the co-occurrence network, thematic map, and annual publication output were significant components. The primary focus of research in this field was AI in 2008, followed by a significant increase between 2020 and 2021 (Fig. 4.2), a decline in 2022, and a recovery in 2023, as evidenced by an analysis of the publication pattern in the sample of extracted articles.

Thematic analysis of the literature, as illustrated in Fig. 4.3, is imperative for the identification of the study's segment. The utilisation of pivotal Industry 4.0 technologies (e.g. AI, machine learning, and ICT) and their potential ramifications on the service sector, encompassing decision-making, catastrophe prevention, and climate change, emerge as predominant themes. The treatment of patients, the function of healthcare professionals, and data analytics are interesting emerging themes that are essential to co-creating value in the healthcare industry. In this context, value co-creation is identified as a pivotal element, as evidenced by the co-occurrence map (Fig. 4.4), which accentuates the pivotal role of AI.

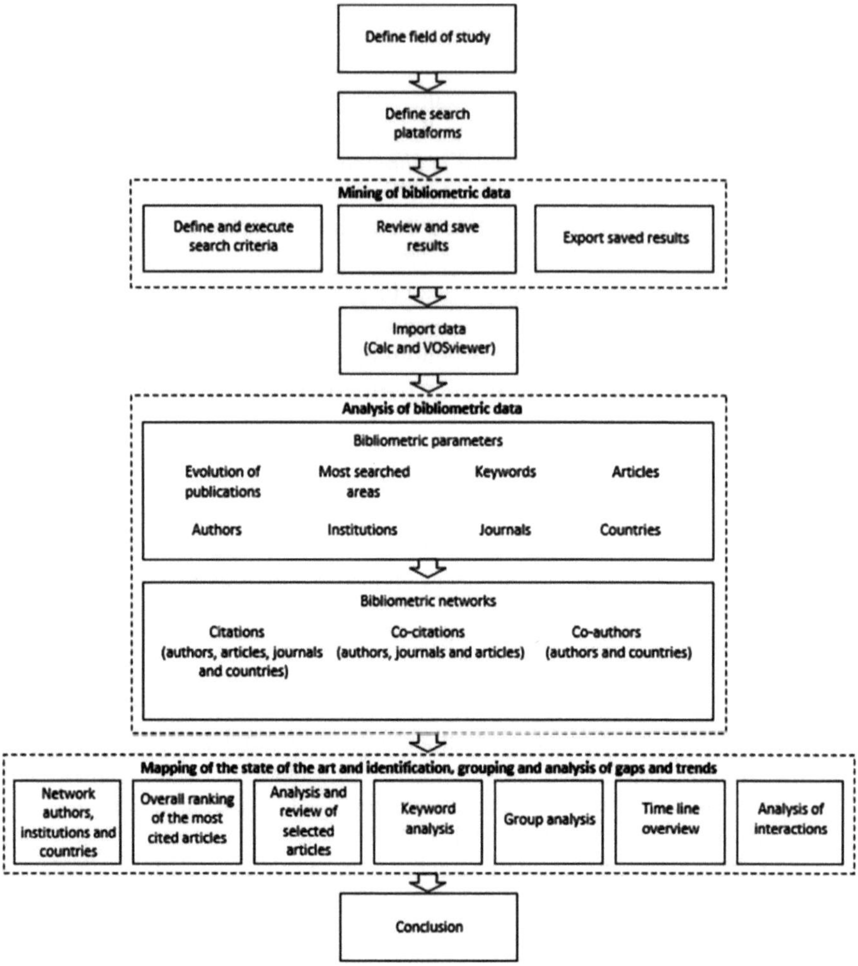

Fig. 4.1 Stages of the method for mapping the state of the art and identifying gaps and trends of research. Source (s): de Oliveira, O. J., da Silva, F. F., Juliani, F., Barbosa, L. C. F. M., & Nunhes, T. V. (2019). Bibliometric method for mapping the state-of-the-art and identifying research gaps and trends in literature: An essential instrument to support the development of scientific projects. In Scientometrics recent advances. IntechOpen

4.5 The Results of the Explorative Analysis

The thematic analysis underlines that GenAI plays a key role in the value creation process within PM networks. First, it catalyses clinical intelligence. Indeed, the integration of digital technologies and GenAI in healthcare has laid the foundation for the emergence of "Smart Health", an innovative care model that powers Internet of Things systems to improve the quality of care. They facilitate real-time health

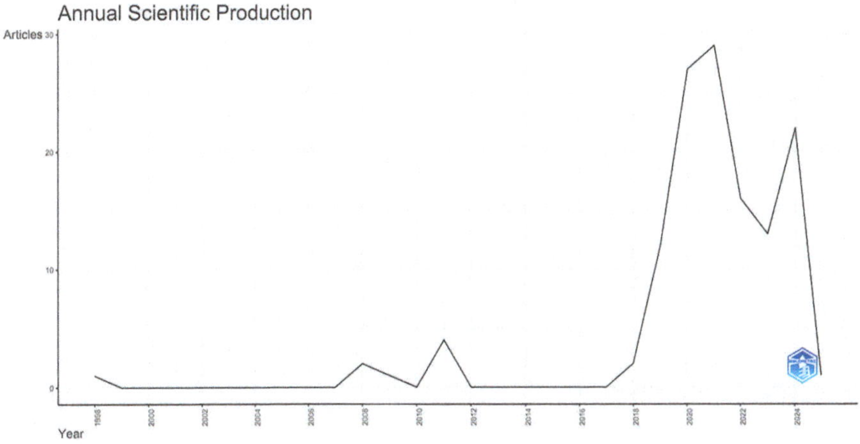

Fig. 4.2 Annual scientific production. Source(s): Bibliometrix output

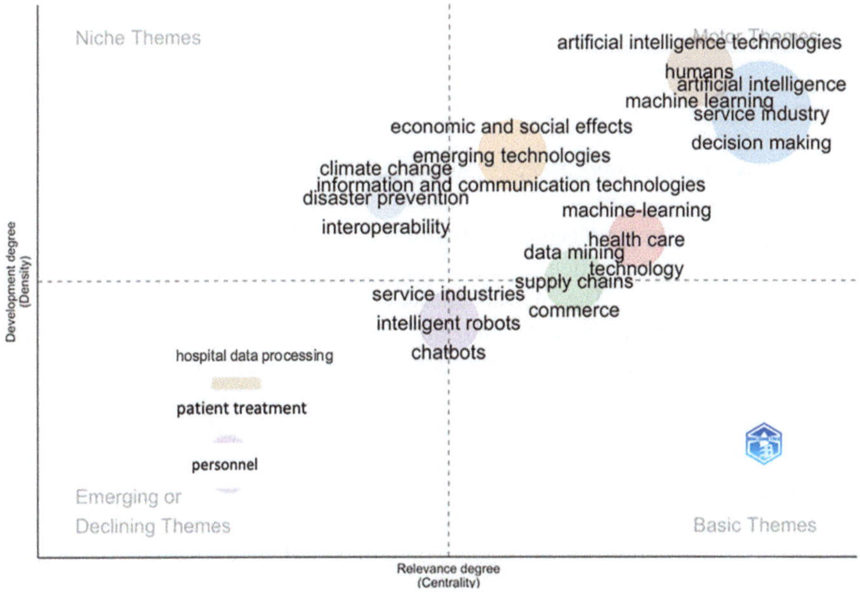

Fig. 4.3 Thematic map. Source(s): Bibliometrix output

data gathering, boosting a connected healthcare ecosystem that brings timely and actionable suggestions to both physicians and patients.

Thus, GenAI proves to be a *game-changer* due to its analytic capability. Particularly, it can process and interpret complex data, offering targeted recommendations that support disease prevention, early diagnosis, and personalised treatment. Furthermore, GenAI is fundamental as a smart data analysis means, generating and

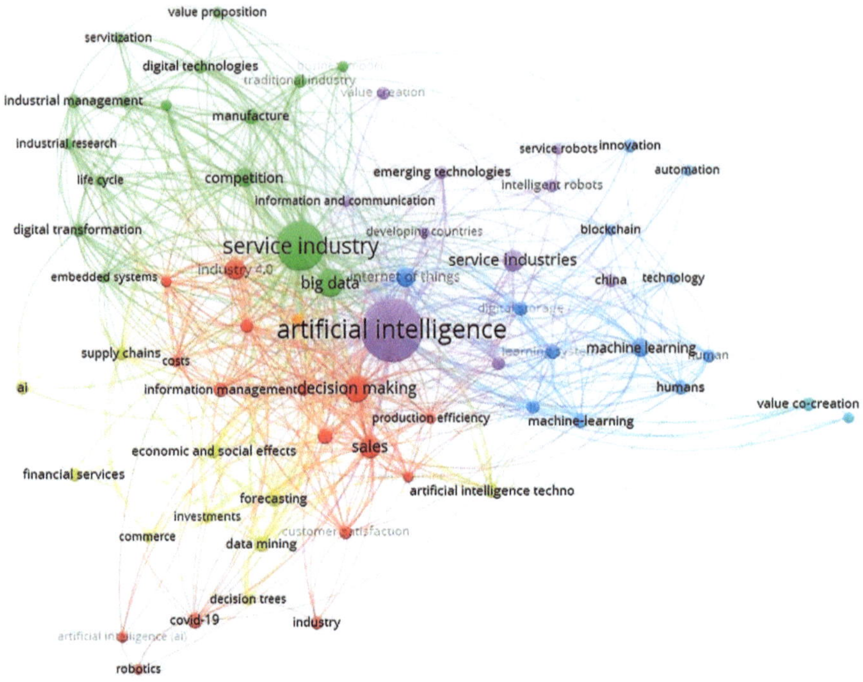

Fig. 4.4 Co-occurrence network. Source(s): Author elaboration

integrating genetic and molecular data with remarkable accuracy and depth. This enables a snapshot of a patient's health and supports more informed and personalised clinical decisions. The analysis attested that healthcare organisations adopting GenAI significantly benefit from enhanced operational efficiency, analysis accuracy, and adaptability in managing data. Particularly, in the PM, GenAI accelerates relevant genetic combinations identification, decreasing the time required to analyse a huge genetic dataset and easing faster diagnosis and effective therapies development.

Despite its potential, GenAI is not without risks, that is, transparency and reliability of its output. Because GenAI models often rely on complex and opaque algorithms, they can produce a *"black box"* effect, reducing trust in the outputs' reliability and fostering over-reliance on them. Thus, ongoing monitoring of GenAI results is crucial to ensure transparency and reliability. Human supervision plays a pivotal role in this process. Indeed, appropriate supervision helps in reducing algorithmic biases, which can lead to discriminatory outputs, exacerbating social inequalities. Therefore, such biases can pose a barrier to a more equitable and inclusive healthcare system. To avoid such risks, healthcare professionals must be adequately educated in developing representative and unbiased training datasets. In addition, clear guidelines and a regulatory framework are needed to support the responsible GenAI implementation.

Lastly, GenAI acts as a bridge to a human-centred care model. Patients are not only passive receivers of care but as active actors in the value co-creation. Thus, patient involvement and empowerment are crucial. In this context, GenAI has the potential to support the transition from volume-oriented healthcare to one focused on human needs, where individuals are the core of the decision-making process. Putting humans at the centre is not limited to patients; it includes healthcare professionals. Thus, to stimulate innovation, it is essential to equip healthcare professionals with the appropriate tools that foster interdisciplinary communication and collaboration.

4.6 Generative AI as a Catalyst for Value Co-creation

Through the empirical analysis, the author developed a new conceptual framework (Fig. 4.5) to map the potential impact of GenAI on the value co-creation process within the healthcare ecosystem. As stated in Chap. 3, defining a value-driven and digitally oriented healthcare ecosystem presupposes a continuous learning process (Friedman et al., 2015), stimulated by six main pillars aligned and interconnected with a view to maximising value. Technology plays a key role (Menear et al., 2019). Embracing digital technologies, therefore, is crucial to stimulate a virtuous circle in which the interaction and collaboration among stakeholders foster continuous learning. Embedding this learning into daily practice leads to the spread of knowledge and value creation (Brooks et al., 2017; Polese et al., 2021; Van den Broek et al., 2018; Vargo & Lusch, 2014).

To develop the conceptual framework, a three-tiered structure—*macro, meso* and *micro*—was adopted to snapshot the complexity of health systems while emphasising the interconnections between the different dimensions of the value co-creation process, the actors engaged and the main goals to be achieved (Menear et al., 2019). Besides, the value co-creation process in PM is defined based on Denicolai and Previtali's (2020) research, who figure four interrelated and interdependent stages: (1) prevention, (2) diagnosis, (3) optimisation, and (4) monitoring.

Thus, the proposed framework identifies specific goals at each level oriented to co-creating value. GenAI supports the achievement of goals either through direct intervention or indirect support. Furthermore, they are interconnected, connecting the levels. Thus, achieving one goal can positively influence the success of the others based on a continuous process of feedback and learning. This process aims to optimise efficiency, personalisation of treatments, as well as collaboration among actors (Fui-Hoon Nah et al., 2023; Ruiz-Rojas et al., 2024).

At the *micro level*, GenAI acts as a driver of operational efficiency. Its capacity to gather and analyse huge amounts of data enables the integration of genomic and molecular data across different facilities, encouraging the formation of collaborative networks (Moulaei et al., 2024; Reddy, 2024). These technologies also provide healthcare professionals with real-time access to multiple genetic combinations, ensuring more precise and accurate diagnoses (Doron et al., 2023, 2025; Sai et al.,

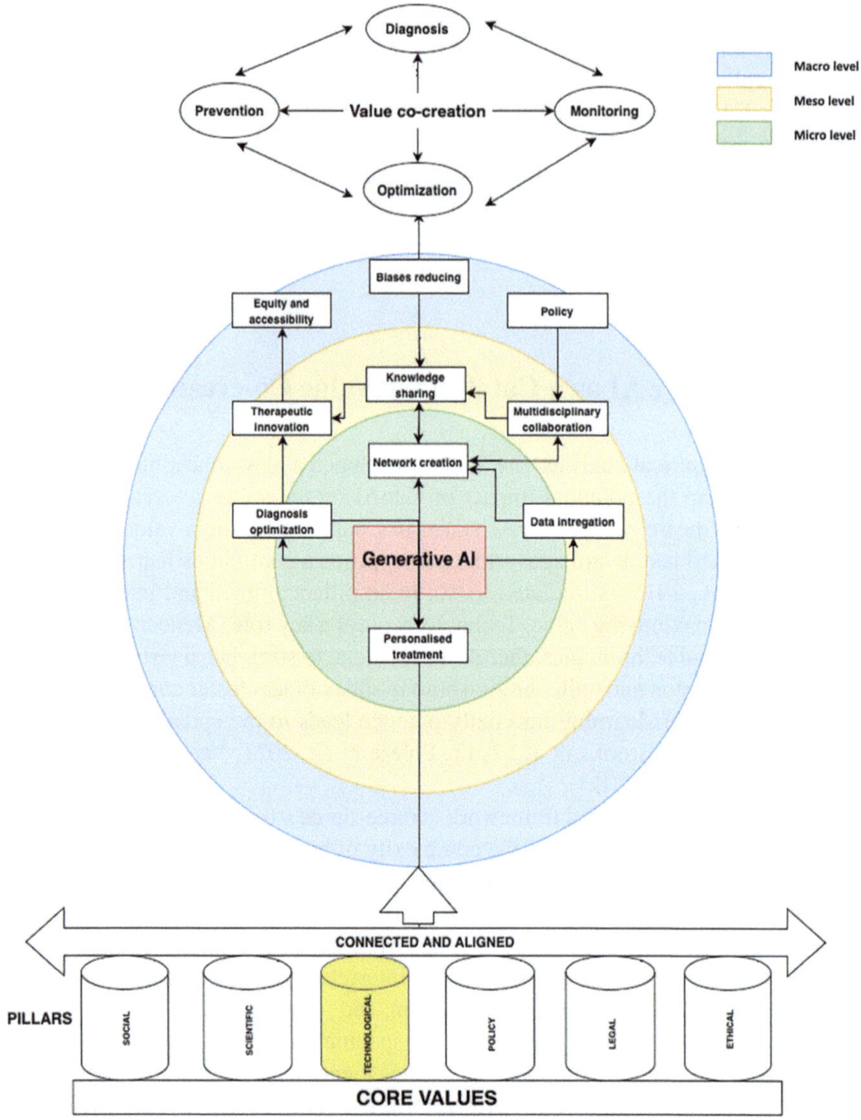

Fig. 4.5 Conceptual framework about Generative AI as a catalyst for value co-creation. Source(s): Author's research

2024; Zhang & Kamel Boulos, 2023). This turns into a highly personalised therapeutic approach tailored to the specific needs of each patient (Yim et al., 2024). Thus, patient engagement in therapeutic decision-making becomes critical, contributing to better patient experience and improved clinical outcomes. Indeed, by adopting a value-based approach (Porter, 2006), patients' participation is, therefore, fundamental to shaping human-centred healthcare systems and personalising treatment protocols (Buccoliero, 2010). This is relevant in PM, where individual patient characteristics drive professionals in selecting the most appropriate therapies.

At the *meso level*, developing multidisciplinary collaboration among actors—for example, hospitals, research centres, the pharmaceutical industry, and patients—is key to stimulating standardised protocols and improving clinical practices constantly through knowledge sharing. So, GenAI could act as a powerful tool supporting information exchange, streamlining communication, and fostering therapeutic innovation.

Finally, at the *macro level*, value maximisation depends on precise health policies that stimulate fair access to care, ensure health data protection, and address potential biases. In this context, GenAI could support genomic and clinical data management on a large scale, serving the optimisation of healthcare resource allocation and enhancing transparency (Gupta et al., 2020; Marques & Ferreira, 2020). Nevertheless, its implementation must be ruled by human supervision to ensure fair outcomes and patient privacy (Ghassemi & Nsoesie, 2022; O'Neil, 2017). The sensitivity of healthcare data, thus, makes the massive use of digital technologies risky to patient safety (Cavacece et al., 2022; Quach et al., 2022; Russo-Spena et al., 2019, 2022; Yang et al., 2019). Therefore, it is fundamental for policymakers at the macro level to establish clear guidelines for the adoption of such technologies and a monitoring system to measure their impact and effectiveness. These mechanisms help in identifying potential bottlenecks and mitigating biases in the training datasets.

Furthermore, a core element of the conceptual framework is the interconnectedness between the different levels, ensuring a continuous flow of information and learning across them. Macro-level policies and guidelines inform the meso-level practices, promoting cooperation among institutions and actors. This enhances operational procedures at the micro level. Simultaneously, insights from the micro level feed into the meso level, contributing to a virtuous cycle of collaboration, knowledge sharing, and innovation.

4.7 Conclusions and Implications

The co-creation of value and its evolution in the digital age is a key challenge within the current academic debate. Among several digital technologies shaping this phenomenon, GenAI is a promising driver of innovation across several sectors, due to its analytical and predictive capabilities.

In manufacturing, for instance, GenAI is used to monitor and optimise production processes, identifying defects in real time and minimising the possibility of human error, supporting decision-making. As discussed before, in healthcare, it has the potential to improve patient care, revolutionising the diagnostic process.

Despite the growing interest in technological and architectural features of GenAI, management literature still lacks a deeper understanding of its potential impact on the value co-creation process within inter-organisational networks in the service industry. To bridge the gap, this book proposes a conceptual framework that qualifies GenAI as a catalyst of value co-creation across three interrelated levels—*macro, meso, and micro*—within PM ecosystems. From an ecosystem perspective, GenAI is not a stand-alone enabler, but its effectiveness depends on data quality, human supervision, bias mitigation, and the ethical safeguards. It is more evident in a highly regulated sector, such as healthcare.

The conceptual framework and the exploratory nature of the study laid the ground for the development of a research agenda to drive future empirical investigation (Table 4.4).

This book provides valuable insights into both theory and practice, opening the way to future research. From a theoretical standpoint, it enriches academic debate on innovation and technological change management in inter-organisational networks. From a managerial perspective, the results highlight the central role of GenAI in improving the quality of care, optimising resource allocation and containing costs. Furthermore, the conceptual framework could help in mapping the critical stages of the value co-creation process, emphasising the enabling factors and barriers that influence the adoption of GenAI within such networks. Lastly, this book could offer food for thought for policymakers, encouraging them to support the adoption of digital technologies through operational guidelines. This could contribute to the development of more resilient and value-driven healthcare networks.

This study is not without limitations due to its qualitative nature, limiting the generalisability of the results. Future studies could integrate quantitative data, allowing predictions and scenarios about the impact of GenAI in the health sector. Additionally, the heterogeneity of national healthcare systems and cultural differences make the results context-specific. Thus, future research could focus on cross-country analysis to offer a broader perspective on the risks and benefits of GenAI.

On the other hand, future research could investigate each level of the conceptual framework to highlight the practical and ethical implications of technologies' implementation. Finally, longitudinal studies could explore the long-term impact and sustainability of integrating GenAI into healthcare systems.

Table 4.4 Research agenda

Level of analysis	Research question
Micro level	How does GenAI affect the role of professionals within the ecosystem?
	How does using GenAI enhance patient engagement in value co-creation?
Meso level	How does GenAI contribute to more equitable access to care?
	Which regulatory frameworks effectively identify and mitigate biases in GenAI models?
Macro level	How does trust among stakeholders influence the adoption of GenAI?
	How does GenAI promote collaboration and standardisation in inter-organisational networks?

Source(s): Author's research

References

Aria, M., & Cuccurullo, C. (2017). bibliometrix: An R-tool for comprehensive science mapping analysis. *Journal of Informetrics, 11*(4), 959–975.

Bogner, A., Littig, B., & Menz, W. (2009). Introduction: Expert interviews—An introduction to a new methodological debate. In *Interviewing experts* (pp. 1–13). Palgrave Macmillan.

Braun, V., & Clarke, V. (2006). Using thematic analysis in psychology. *Qualitative Research in Psychology, 3*(2), 77–101.

Brooks, D., Douglas, M., Aggarwal, N., Prabhakaran, S., Holden, K., & Mack, D. (2017). Developing a framework for integrating health equity into the learning health system. *Learning Health Systems, 1*(3), e10029.

Buccoliero, L. (2010). E-health 2.0. Tecnologie per il patient empowerment. *Mondo Digitale, 4*, 3–17.

Campbell, D., Picard-Aitken, M., Côté, G., Caruso, J., Valentim, R., Edmonds, S., Macaluso, B., Robitaille, J.-P., Bastien, N., Laframboise, M.-C., Lebeau, L.-M., Mirabel, P., Larivière, V., & Archambault, É. (2010). Bibliometrics as a performance measurement tool for research evaluation: The case of research funded by the National Cancer Institute of Canada. *American Journal of Evaluation, 31*(1), 66–83.

Cavacece, Y., Ebraico, S., Spena, T. R., Mele, C., Leone, D., Schiavone, F., & Bastone, A. (2022, October). Blockchain technology and artificial intelligence for value co-creation in healthcare. In *2022 IEEE international conference on metrology for extended reality, artificial intelligence and neural engineering (MetroXRAINE)* (pp. 522–527). IEEE.

Charmaz, K. (2008). Reconstructing grounded theory. In P. Alasuutari, L. Bickman, & J. Brannen (Eds.), *The Sage handbook of social research methods* (pp. 461–478). Sage.

Charmaz, K. (2015). Teaching theory construction with initial grounded theory tools: A reflection on lessons and learning. *Qualitative Health Research, 25*(12), 1610–1622

Cohen, L., Manion, L., & Morrison, K. (2002). Research methods in education. *Commercialize Complex Goods. Strategic Management Journal, 17*, 169–195. Routledge.

Denicolai, S., & Previtali, P. (2020). Precision medicine: Implications for value chains and business models in life sciences. *Technological Forecasting and Social Change, 151*, 119767.

de Oliveira, O. J., da Silva, F. F., Juliani, F., Barbosa, L. C. F. M., & Nunhes, T. V. (2019). Bibliometric method for mapping the state-of-the-art and identifying research gaps and trends in literature: An essential instrument to support the development of scientific projects. In S. Kunosic & E. Zerem (Eds.), *Scientometrics recent advances*. IntechOpen.

Doron, G., Genway, S., Roberts, M., & Jasti, S. (2023). New horizons: Pioneering pharmaceutical R&D with Generative AI from lab to the clinic—An industry perspective. *arXiv Preprint*. https://doi.org/10.48550/arXiv.2312.12482

Doron, G., Genway, S., Roberts, M., & Jasti, S. (2025). Generative AI: Driving productivity and scientific breakthroughs in pharmaceutical R&D. *Drug Discovery Today, 30*(1), 104272.

Friedman, C., Rubin, J., Brown, J., Buntin, M., Corn, M., Etheredge, L., Gunter, C., Musen, M., Platt, R., Stead, W., Sullivan, K., & Van Houweling, D. (2015). Toward a science of learning systems: a research agenda for the high-functioning Learning Health System. *Journal of the American Medical Informatics Association, 22*(1), 43–50.

Fui-Hoon Nah, F., Zheng, R., Cai, J., Siau, K., & Chen, L. (2023). Generative AI and ChatGPT: Applications, challenges, and AI-human collaboration. *Journal of Information Technology Case and Application Research, 25*(3), 277–304.

Ghassemi, M., & Nsoesie, E. O. (2022). In medicine, how do we machine learn anything real? *Patterns, 3*(1).

Gläser, J., & Laudel, G. (2015). A bibliometric reconstruction of research trails for qualitative investigations of scientific innovations. *Historical Social Research/Historische Sozialforschung, 40*(3), 299–330.

Gupta, S., Leszkiewicz, A., Kumar, V., Bijmolt, T., & Potapov, D. (2020). Digital analytics: Modeling for insights and new methods. *Journal of Interactive Marketing, 51*(1), 26–43.

Joffe, H. (2011). Thematic analysis. In D. Harper & A. R. Thompson (Eds.), *Qualitative research methods in mental health and psychotherapy: A guide for students and practitioners* (pp. 209–223). Wiley.

Lokot, M. (2021). Whose voices? Whose knowledge? A feminist analysis of the value of key informant interviews. *International Journal of Qualitative Methods, 20*, 1609406920948775.

Marques, I. C., & Ferreira, J. J. (2020). Digital transformation in the area of health: systematic review of 45 years of evolution. *Health and Technology, 10*(3), 575–586.

Menear, M., Blanchette, M. A., Demers-Payette, O., & Roy, D. (2019). A framework for value-creating learning health systems. *Health Research Policy and Systems, 17*, 1–13.

Moulaei, K., Yadegari, A., Baharestani, M., Farzanbakhsh, S., Sabet, B., & Afrash, M. R. (2024). Generative artificial intelligence in healthcare: A scoping review on benefits, challenges and applications. *International Journal of Medical Informatics, 188*, 105474.

Naderifar, M., Goli, H., & Ghaljaie, F. (2017). Snowball sampling: A purposeful method of sampling in qualitative research. *Strides in Development of Medical Education, 14*(3).

O'Neil, C. (2017). *Weapons of math destruction: How big data increases inequality and threatens democracy*. Crown.

Pahwa, M., Cavanagh, A., & Vanstone, M. (2023). Key informants in applied qualitative health research. *Qualitative Health Research, 33*(14), 1251–1261.

Parker, C., Scott, S., & Geddes, A. (2019). Snowball sampling. In P. Atkinson, S. Delamont, A. Cernat, J. W. Sakshaug, & R. A. Williams (Eds.), *Sage research methods foundations*. Sage.

Polese, F., Troisi, O., Grimaldi, M., & Loia, F. (2021). Reinterpreting governance in smart cities: an ecosystem-based view. In A. Visvizi & R. P. del Hoyo (Eds.), *Smart cities and the UN SDGs* (pp. 71–89). Elsevier.

Porter, M. E. (2006). *Redefining health care: creating value-based competition on results*. Harvard Business Press.

Pranckutė, R. (2021). Web of science (WoS) and scopus: The titans of bibliographic information in today's academic world. *Publications, 9*(1), 12.

Quach, S., Thaichon, P., Martin, K. D., Weaven, S., & Palmatier, R. W. (2022). Digital technologies: tensions in privacy and data. *Journal of the Academy of Marketing Science, 50*(6), 1299–1323.

Reddy, S. (2024). Generative AI in healthcare: an implementation science informed translational path on application, integration and governance. *Implementation Science, 19*(1), 27.

Ruiz-Rojas, L. I., Salvador-Ullauri, L., & Acosta-Vargas, P. (2024). Collaborative working and critical thinking: Adoption of generative artificial intelligence tools in higher education. *Sustainability, 16*(13), 5367.

Russo-Spena, T., Mele, C., Cavacece, Y., Ebraico, S., Dantas, C., Roseiro, P., & van Staalduinen, W. (2022). Enabling value co-creation in healthcare through blockchain technology. *International Journal of Environmental Research and Public Health, 20*(1), 67.

Russo-Spena, T., Mele, C., & Marzullo, M. (2019). Practising value innovation through artificial intelligence: the IBM Watson case. *Journal of Creating Value, 5*(1), 11–24.

Sai, S., Gaur, A., Sai, R., Chamola, V., Guizani, M., & Rodrigues, J. J. (2024). *Generative AI for transformative healthcare: A comprehensive study of emerging models, applications, case studies and limitations*. IEEE Access.

Suri, H. (2011). Purposeful sampling in qualitative research synbook. *Qualitative Research Journal, 11*(2), 63–75.

Taylor, G. A., & Blake, B. J. (2015). Key informant interviews and focus groups. In M. de Chesnay (Ed.), *Nursing research using data analysis: Qualitative designs and methods in nursing* (pp. 153–165). Springer.

Van den Broek, J., Boselie, P., & Paauwe, J. (2018). Cooperative innovation through a talent management pool: A qualitative study on coopetition in healthcare. *European Management Journal, 36*(1), 135–144.

Vargo, S. L., & Lusch, R. F. (2014). Inversions of service-dominant logic. *Marketing Theory, 14*(3), 239–248.

Yang, Y., Zheng, X., Guo, W., Liu, X., & Chang, V. (2019). Privacy-preserving smart IoT-based healthcare big data storage and self-adaptive access control system. *Information Sciences, 479*, 567–592.

Yim, D., Khuntia, J., Parameswaran, V., & Meyers, A. (2024). Preliminary evidence of the use of Generative AI in health care clinical services: Systematic narrative review. *JMIR Medical Informatics, 12*(1), e52073.

Yin, R. K. (2009). *Case study research: Design and methods* (Vol. 5). Sage.

Zhang, P., & Kamel Boulos, M. N. (2023). Generative AI in medicine and healthcare: promises, opportunities and challenges. *Future Internet, 15*(9), 286.

MIX
Papier aus verantwortungsvollen Quellen
Paper from responsible sources
FSC® C105338

If you have any concerns about our products,
you can contact us on
ProductSafety@springernature.com

In case Publisher is established outside the EU,
the EU authorized representative is:
Springer Nature Customer Service Center GmbH
Europaplatz 3, 69115 Heidelberg, Germany

Printed by Libri Plureos GmbH
in Hamburg, Germany